A SCORPION'S LAIR

A SCORPION'S LAIR

JOKERS GONE WILD
(VOLUME 2)

EARNESTINE M. WALDEN

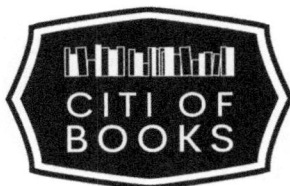

CITI OF BOOKS

CITIOFBOOKS, INC.
3736 Eubank NE Suite A1
Albuquerque, NM 87111-3579
www.citiofbooks.com
Hotline: 1 (877) 389-2759
Fax: 1 (505) 930-7244

Ordering Information:

Quantity sales. Special discounts are available on quantity purchases by corporations, associations, and others. For details, contact the publisher at the address above.

Printed in the United States of America.

ISBN-13:   Softcover   978-1-960952-89-9

Library of Congress Control Number: 2023913587

As he stood knocking on the door, a gruff voice from within yelled, "Come on in, it's open!"

"Hey, Brad, have a chair. I'll be with you in a couple of minutes." He sat quietly as the big burly man sitting behind the desk began placing papers in a number of folders, then moving them to the side. Having completed the task and leaning back in his chair, he looked at Bradford, smiled, and said, "I see you finally made it back. Good news this time, I hope." "I'm inclined to believe so," he said, returning the smile.

"Kendall, during my last visit here I couldn't go into details with you because the investigation was still in progress."

"Yes, something about having to tie up some loose ends?" "Affirmative," he replied with a grin.

"And the loose ends—they're all tied up, I presume."

"Your presumption is correct. You see, this whole episode was about greed and revenge."

"Greed and revenge?"

"Yes, with Carrington it was greed. He reneged on an agreement between David Lansing and himself and lost all of his authority in the firm. Steven Chatsworth had been planning for years on how he would destroy Lansing as the result of something that had transpired years ago. When Carrington went to him for assistance in his little scheme, it opened the door of opportunity that he had been waiting for. By stirring up trouble among the contractor's companies to divert attention away from the true motive, no one would realize what was happening until it was too late, including Carrington himself. Because of his greed, he only sought to gain control of the firm from Claudia with Chatsworth's help, whereas Chatsworth wanted it destroyed."

"But why would he want to destroy the firm?"

"His words were, 'It represented David Lansing himself.'"

"But Brad, I always assumed he and Lansing to have been close friends, and so did everyone else who knew them."

"That's the ironic part about it, Kendall; he planned it that way so he would be above suspicion if his plan had succeeded." "Shakespeare's beard!" he exclaimed.

"What's going to happen now that it's over?"

"Well, I wouldn't worry about Carrington getting into any more mischief, and as for Chatsworth," he paused, then said, "with a man like him it's difficult to say. Maybe now everyone has learned a lesson from all of this with a broad grin."

"Man, I for one have. From now on I'm going to initiate a thorough background check on all of my perspective employees." They both laughed heartily. Then Bradford's expression changed to a more serious one when he asked, "Kendall, have you had the opportunity to visit Brandt?"

"Yes, as a matter of fact, I was there last night. He's doing about as well as can be expected under the circumstances. He's going to be placed in a skilled nursing care facility and the guys have set up a financial fund to help defray some of the medical costs."

"Kendall, I think that's just great."

"By the way, a meeting was held for all of the companies who wanted to attend, both small and large. You opened our eyes to what it really means by fair competition, and we owe you a big debt of gratitude for which we can never repay, Brad."

Bradford stood up, as did Kendall, and Brad said, "I'm only glad to have been of help."

Kendall looked at him, smiled and said, "You have been. Thanks, Brad."

Returning the smile, he said, "You're more than welcome, Kendall," as they shook hands. After he had driven a short distance away from the construction site, his car phone rang. Answering, he said, "This is Maxwell."

The voice on the other end said, "Brad, this is Blake. I've been trying to reach you for quite some time."

"What's the matter, Blake?"

"The authorities are out at Chatsworth's residence. It appears he's been shot several times."

"What? When did this happen, Blake?"

"From what I've been able to learn so far, it was around the time we were meeting here with Charles."

"Did they say how he was shot and by whom?"

"No. They're speaking with his housekeeper now, and from what I understand, she heard some gunshots, found him lying on the floor bleeding and called the authorities."

"This is terrible, even for a man like him. At this stage, you're probably not going to get much information, but perhaps you might continue to see what else you'll be able to learn." After a short pause, he said, "Look, Blake, I'll be in your office shortly." While still driving, Bradford was recalling the previous day's event at Chatsworth's home and said, "Something is not right about any of this. I wonder if my earlier suspicion is correct."

Bradford arrived at Blake's office within half an hour after their conversation and was immediately apprised of the latest information on Steven Chatsworth. As they sat in his office watching a special newscast on television announcing the recent developments in the Chatsworth case, Bradford wondered to himself if his suspicion was warranted. Since the investigation was ongoing, certain information was being withheld. A hospital spokesman for the medical team stated that his condition was guarded and would be updated periodically as warranted. A spokesman for the Santa Monica police department made a brief statement saying they were searching for three of Chatsworth's employees for questioning in the matter.

Blake turned the set-off and leaned back in his chair, then asked, "Brad, what could have possibly happened out there?"

His direct response to Blake's question was, "I don't know, Blake, but there's one thing for certain—it was violent enough for Chatsworth to end up in the hospital seriously wounded. The authorities never gave the names of the three employees, but I'll bet you a ten-dollar gold piece that I can give you the name of one."

Blake looked at him for a full minute, then asked, "Brad, just what do you mean?"

He was all too familiar with that facial expression when Bradford leaned forward and said, "Doing my last meeting with Chatsworth, I informed him that the authorities had been notified regarding the assault against Phillip Brandt by his men. Blake, do you recall my telling you that?"

I observed the expression on their faces when he told them to get out of his sight and stay out. The one in particular called Joker had a sneaky grin on his face."

"Yes, I do recall your telling me and you also said with great certainty that he was up to something."

"Wait a minute, are you implying that he could be one of the three involved in this incident?"

"Blake, I honestly believe so."

"But why? What could possibly be the motive behind it?"

Bradford leaned back in his chair, crossed his legs, and with eyes focused directly on Blake, saying, "Let's look at it from this perspective. Say, for instance, he was the right-hand man. Chatsworth gave the orders, but he made sure they were carried out, and all of the incidents that occurred he was present with the exception of two. Once at the contractor's meeting and the first time I paid a visit to Chatsworth's home. When he told the two to get out, he specifically said, "The three of you." Suddenly, his usefulness and importance had ended—now where did that leave him? Wouldn't you become bitter and resentful of the man who caused you to lose face in front of the others?"

Blake sat gazing at him for a while and said, "Looking at it from that point of view, Brad, I'm inclined to agree with you on both accounts. But there's one thing that's puzzling to me." "What is that?" he asked him.

"Why go back to his residence after having been told on no uncertain terms to stay out?"

"I don't know. Perhaps to use someone else as a scapegoat in bargaining for his position back. Blake, it's difficult to say what could be going on in the mind of a person like Joker."

"That's true, and if your assessment of him is correct, they're not going to stick around waiting for the authorities to get their hands on them, then I'm afraid they will become fugitives from justice." Blake had barely finished speaking when the telephone on his desk rang. Immediately picking it up, he asked, "Yes, Jenny?"

"Mr. Colwell, excuse me, sir, but a detective name Jacob Skylar with the Santa Monica Police Department is on the other line and wishes to speak with you."

"Thank you, Jenny, please put him through." Looking directly at Bradford, he said, "This is Attorney Blake Colwell speaking."

"Attorney Colwell, my name is Jacob Skylar. I'm with the Santa Monica Police Department. I've been assigned as investigator in the Chatsworth case."

"How may I be of assistance to you, Detective?"

"I understand you know Mr. Chatsworth?"

"Yes, that is correct." There was a brief pause, then he asked, "Attorney Colwell, there are a few questions I'd like to ask you. Would

it inconvenience you if I could come to your office today?"

"No, not at all! What time will you be able to come?"

Apparently looking at the time, he spoke and said, "It's now ten fifteen; how about eleven o'clock?"

"Eleven o'clock will be fine. Do you know where my office is located?" "Yes, I do, and thank you for taking the time to speak with me."

"You're welcome, Detective." He looked at Bradford and said, "He wants to ask me some questions regarding Steven Chatsworth." Bradford smiled and said, "That's great. Perhaps we can learn something else. In the meanwhile, I've got a couple of errands to run, so I'll get back with you later. You know how you can reach me if something else comes up."

"Yes, I do."

"Yes, Jenny?"

"Detective Skylar is here to see you, sir."

"Thank you, Jenny, please send him in."

"Yes, sir." Blake was standing up behind his desk closing some folders when the detective entered the door. He looked up at the man as he came towards him with an extended hand and introducing himself. Blake shook his hand and asked him to have a seat. "Now, what would you like to know, Detective?"

"Attorney Blake, I'm going to get right to the point. How long have you known Mr. Chatsworth?"

"I really appreciate that, Detective, and to answer your question I've known him for many years."

"And how long have you represented the Lansing contractor's firm?"

"I've been their attorney for over thirty years."

"I see." Now Blake's inner thoughts were, what is he leading up to?

"The firm has been involved in a business scandal since the deaths of its owners, am I correct?"

"Yes, you're quite correct. Was Mr. Chatsworth associated with the firm in any way?" Blake stared at the man before speaking then he asked Detective Skylar, just what is this line of questioning leading up to?"

"Attorney Colwell, I'm investigating an attempted murder case here and that entails covering all bases."

"I understand your position perfectly well, but have you had the opportunity to question Mr. Chatsworth's position regarding the contractor's firm?"

He looked at Blake and said, "No, I haven't."

"Then I believe that is a question best answered by Chatsworth himself."

Skylar gave him a sullen look and said, "I see." Looking directly at Blake, he asked, "The daughter inherited the business after her folk's deaths, didn't she?"

"Yes, she did," was his immediate response to Skylar's question. At that moment, Blake knew he was changing in midstream and smiled inwardly. "Isn't she married?" he asked him.

"Yes, she is."

"What about the husband?"

"What about him?"

"Does he share in any of the business?"

"No, he doesn't, he's the structural engineer in the firm and that is it."

"I see," he said resolutely. "Incidentally, I understand a private investigator was hired to look into the situation."

"That's correct. His name is Bradford T. Maxwell."

"Has he made any progress?"

Smiling, Blake responded, "I believe he has." As a matter of fact, I believe it just might be advantageous for you to speak with him." He gave him a blank stare and asked, "Why do you believe that?"

"Because he might be in a position to assist you more than I."

"Is that a fact?"

"Yes, it is."

"Where can I reach this Maxwell fellow?" He laughed and gave him a sheet of paper from his notepad with Bradford's name, address and telephone number written on it. Taking the paper and standing up, he said, "Thanks for your time, Attorney Colwell."

"You're welcome, Detective Skylar."

He'd just gotten into his car when the phone rang and looking at the display, he said, "Hello, Blake, what is it?"

"Brad, Detective Skylar just left my office. I gave him your office telephone number and address. I believe you should expect a visit from him soon." Pausing for a brief minute and with a wide smile, he asked him, "Oh, and why is that, Blake?"

"For two reasons, Brad. Number one, he asked if Chatsworth is associated with the firm in any way."

"What did you tell him?"

"I asked if he'd had the opportunity to question him regarding his position in the firm and he said no. Then I told him I believe that is a question best answered by Chatsworth himself." "And number two?" Bradford asked him.

"He's aware that you're investigating the situation involving the firm and asked if you've made any progress. I merely told him I believe so. As a matter of fact, I assured him that it might be more advantageous for him to speak with you."

"Oh, you did, did you?" he asked, laughing.

"Look, Brad, we know Chatsworth was the mastermind behind the whole incident, but I believe it's up to you to inform him of how much of it you want him to know right now. Besides, if your assessment of the incident that occurred at Chatsworth's home is correct, he can probably use your assistance in this present matter."

"You just might be right, buddy, but we'll see what develops when he comes to see me. I'm on my way back to the office anyway. So, I'll be in touch with you later." The conversation with Bradford concluded.

Blake's thoughts were of Chatsworth and his ties with the firm, which were not publicly known. That was an agreement between he and David Lansing years ago before he came to the firm. Since things had taken such a dramatic change, including his having masterminded the whole situation, he wondered to himself what decision he would be making after his recovery. As of the moment, Claudia still was not aware of the role he had played in the pickle situation, nor the full extent of Charles's involvement in all of it.

She will be returning from abroad in a few days. Perhaps by the time she does return here, things will be completely resolved, at least. I hope they will be.

Maxwell was sitting behind his desk going over some paperwork when he heard a knock on his door. Looking up in the direction of the sound, he said, "Come in, it's open," while slowly moving back away from the desk. Just as he stood up, a man nearly as tall as he was coming through the door. The man appeared to have been in his early forties, with a tan that might have indicated he was an avid surfer, reddish-brown hair and hazel eyes. Suddenly, they both began laughing. Apparently, he was sizing Maxwell up as well. Finally, he said, "I'm Detective Jacob Skylar with the Santa Monica Police Department."

"And I'm Bradford T. Maxwell." They shook hands and Maxwell asked him to have a seat. "Now, what can I do for you, Detective Skylar?"

"I've been assigned to investigate an attempted murder case. I spoke with Attorney Blake Colwell this morning and his suggestion was that it would be to my advantage too if I spoke with you. To be perfectly honest with you, I was somewhat skeptical of his suggestion until I reported to my supervisor informing him that I was on my way to see you. Then he told me under no uncertain terms that I should have contacted you first." "And why is that?"

"He informed me that you're the man who notified the department of an assault on a man by three men who is employed by Steven Chatsworth, the case I'm now investigating."

"The first part of your statement is correct."

"What'd you mean by the first part?"

"At the time of the assault they were in his employment, but when I informed him of what happened he point blank told the three to get out of his sight and stay out."

Upon hearing that statement, a puzzled expression appeared on Skylar's face. He asked, "How did you know they worked for Chatsworth anyway?"

"I was investigating a case when the victim suddenly disappeared from his post."

"What do you mean?"

"He worked as a dispatcher for one of the larger construction companies."

"How did you learn about his disappearance?"

"I was in the office with the employer when he called the dispatch office. When there was no response, he sent one of his men to search for him, and when he returned there was no dispatcher with him, and all of the records were missing as well."

By this time, Detective Skylar appeared to be more comfortable talking with him. Maxwell leaned back in his chair for comfort as well. "Well, Maxwell, what happened after that?"

"I asked the owner a few more questions about the missing man. Then I asked if he had a current address on him. He wrote it down on a piece of paper and gave it to me and I gave him my word that I would try to locate the missing man. Early the following morning I went to the address he had given me. He lived in an apartment complex across town. I went to the apartment number that was supposed to have been his. When there was no response from him, I located the manager and upon questioning him, he told me that he had left the previous day in such a hurry that he left no forwarding address to receive his deposit. Then I asked if he was left alone. He said, 'As a matter of fact, two men accompanied him. From the description he gave me, I knew they were Chatsworth's men'."

"Tell me, how could you have been so certain that they were Chatsworth's men?"

"Because I had met them on three previous occasions; two of them were involved in incidents of harassment." "Against whom?" he asked.

"Maxwell looked at him, smiled and said, "Against me!"

"But why you?"

"I suppose they thought it would intimidate me." "Oh, really?" Skylar asked, smiling.

"Anyway, I found Phillip Brandt the dispatcher about a block away from the apartment complex and he'll never walk again." He gazed at Maxwell for a full minute and said, "Wait a minute, this stuff is getting heavy, Maxwell. What in the devil's name is going on here?"

"It's a long story, Skylar, and the case I'm working on hasn't been resolved yet; now this situation with Chatsworth only complicates things further. I had hoped to close it, but I'll have to wait until he's recovered from his injuries. At least, enough for me to talk to him!" he exclaimed. "Man, out of the frying pan into the fire."

Looking directly into Maxwell's eyes, he asked, "Just what does Chatsworth have to do with any of this in your investigation?"

"Listen, Skylar, I'm not at liberty to divulge every detail at this time, but I can tell you this much and before I do, there are a few questions of my own I'd like to ask you." Skylar stared at him for a very brief time, then said, "All right, what are the questions?"

"First of all, number one, according to the news report the shooting occurred at Chatsworth's residence; is that correct?" "Yes, that's correct," he replied.

"Number two, were there any eyewitnesses to the actual shooting?"

"No."

"What about the housekeeper?"

"What about her?"

"I understand she was questioned?"

"Yes, she was."

"Where was she during this time and what account was she able to give the authorities regarding the incident?" He was hesitant for a couple of seconds, then said, "She stated that she was in the kitchen and heard Chatsworth yell, 'I told you once to get out and stay out, and I meant it. Now what are you doing back here?' Then she heard another man say, 'I want everything you owe me now!' Then he yelled, 'Get out of here!' The next thing that she heard was shots being fired. The poor woman was so frightened that she locked herself in the pantry. And that's where she remained until she heard nothing more and felt it was safe to come out. She stated that when she finally came out, the front door was standing wide open. Then she immediately went to the study and found Chatsworth lying on the floor bleeding. She called out his name a few times, but there was no response she thought he was dead and that's when she managed to make it to the phone and call the police."

"The last question: how many times was he shot and what caliber of gun was used?"

"He was shot once in the chest, twice in the abdomen, and once in the arm. Ballistic reports it as having been a small thirty-eight caliber. Why do you ask, Maxwell?"

"I'll lay you odds ten-to-one I can tell you who did the actual shooting." "How can you be so certain of this?"

"Because the last time I was out there, I had a run-in with the three of them, but only one carried a gun. A man name Joker."

"How do you know this?"

"Because when I sent him skidding between Chatsworth's legs it hit the ground not more than two feet away from him, and it was a thirty-eight special." He leaned forward towards Maxwell and asked, "Exactly when did this take place?"

"A day before the shooting occurred."

"Why are you so certain this Joker is the shooter?"

"The other two are wimps and don't have the nerve. I saw the expression on their faces when he ordered them to get out and stay away. This Joker had a sneaky grin on his face, and I had a gut feeling as I watched them that he'd be up to something sinister."

"After hearing all of this, you just might be right and if you are, I'll guarantee you they're going to be on the run. That is if they haven't fled already because it's been in all the news and television stations that they're wanted for questioning. Listen, I'm still puzzled by something." "What, for instance?" Maxwell asked him.

"Why did Chatsworth's men snatch that fellow anyway?"

"They were supposed to have been following his orders." With a puzzled look on his face, he repeated, "Following his orders?"

"Yes. You see they were told to put him on a plane out of the country but decided to do things their way instead and by so doing, it cost all of them their job. That's why he fired them after learning what they had done. According to Chatsworth, they disobeyed his orders and that wasn't something he would tolerate."

"But why did he want him out of the country in the first place?"

"As a cover-up for what he was doing."

"You mean to tell me that he's involved in something else?"

"Up to his neck in it."

"So, this is why that sly old fox sicced me on you!"

Bradford smiled and said, "Well, Blake Colwell does have a strange way of doing things sometimes."

"This case you're working on—it's the contractor's firm's situation, isn't it?"

"Yes, it is."

"Look, something occurred to me during our conversation." "What is it?" Maxwell asked him.

"I could really use some outside help on this and perhaps it will also help to solve your dilemma." Looking down for a brief minute, then up again, he asked, "How do you see that?"

"Well, as you've stated more or less, you really can't resolve the firm's situation until Chatsworth's recovered, right?"

"Yes, that's true."

"Maxwell, I'm going to be upfront with you."

"I would appreciate that very much," he said, half-smiling.

"When I learned that you're the investigator in the firm's business scandal, I wanted to know something about the man I'd be interviewing. I did some background checking on my own and I must admit I'm very impressed at what I've learned."

Smiling, Bradford gazed at him and asked, "Is that a fact?" Returning the smile, Skylar replied, "Yes, it is. You're a well-known private investigator with a reputation for not only getting the job done, but you're honest and having integrity. This is something I've always admired in a person. Maxwell, I've been on the force for nearly twelve years now and I've seen my share of those who've somehow lost this quality along the way, for whatever reason. And this meeting with you has been validated through our conversation."

"Skylar, people are who they are; it doesn't matter what profession they're in or where they come from."

"You've got a good point there and I fully agree with you. And back to my question, will you at least give it some consideration?" Maxwell gazed into his eyes and said, "Yes, I might do just that!" Suddenly, the telephone on his desk began to ring and, looking in Skylar's direction, he nodded his head, apparently asking to excuse him, while answering, "Hello! This is Bradford T. Maxwell."

"Hello, Brad, this is Blake."

"Blake, what's wrong?"

"Have you seen the most recent news report?"

"No, I've been rather busy this afternoon. What news report are you speaking of?"

"Brad, one of Chatsworth's men was found bleeding to death, but get this, before he died he told the police that he'd been shot by Freddy Sinclaire."

"What! When and where did this shooting take place?"

"Apparently, about an hour ago near the Santa Monica pier."

"All right, Blake, I'm tied up right now, but I'll get back with you and thanks for the info. "After replacing the receiver, he looked at Skylar and said, "Joker's gone wild."

Skylar stared at him in total bewilderment and asked, "What's this, Maxwell?"

Maxwell said, "That was Blake Colwell on the phone. About an hour ago near the Santa Monica pier, one of Chatsworth's men was found critically wounded, but before he died, he told the police that he'd been shot by Freddy Sinclaire, 'the Joker'.

"My word! Who's going to die next at the hands of this maniac," Skylar asked, "if he might use the phone?"

"By all means," Maxwell replied. He knew Skylar was most likely to be calling into the station after all; that was his case. He spoke with his supervisor and received an updated report on the incident and Maxwell knew the case had now developed a new twist. When the murder occurred, it became a homicide and would then be turned over to the homicide division for investigation.

Skylar thanked him for the use of the phone and asked, "What do you say now, Maxwell? Will you help us catch those maniacs?"

Looking directly into his eyes, he asked, "What is your suggestion, Skylar?"

He responded by saying, "Chatsworth's hospitalized and you're the only one who knows what these guys look like. I spoke with my supervisor, and he's agreed for you to go to the crime scene to make identification. This way we'll know which ones to be searching for; will you do it?"

He stared at Skylar for a brief minute and replied, "Yes, I'll go with you."

"Thanks, man."

"You're welcome. I want to see the remaining two off the streets as well."

Smiling, Skylar said, "Then let's go to it." They departed from the underground parking structure each in their own car.

Skylar arrived at the crime scene shortly ahead of Maxwell, who parked his car a short distance away. Observing the draped form on the ground, it was obvious that the coroner hadn't yet arrived. Sometimes it takes hours before they make it to the scene because they're always so busy and, for the most part, understaffed. The crime scene was constantly being monitored by assigned police personnel. People were still mulling around and occasionally one of the officers would have to tell them to step back away from the tape. Understandably, this was being done to preserve the crime scene. It never ceased to amaze him why some people would want to stand, sometimes for hours, staring down upon the lifeless form of another human being. While observing all of the activities, Maxwell hadn't noticed that Skylar was attempting to get his attention. Suddenly, he was making his appearance towards him. He spoke and said, "Maxwell, the information that I received is the guy was shot once in the chest and twice in the back. It appears that he was attempting to escape his attacker. I spoke with my supervisor only explaining that you've had a run-in with the three of them while working on a case, and perhaps you can identify which one of the three he is. At least we'll have a name. He's agreed for you to come inside the perimeter."

"Thanks. Let's go; I'm curious to see which one he was." That's something he never felt quite comfortable with—looking at the still, lifeless form of another human being. They finally reached the area and signaled to proceed on beneath the tape. As they approached the scene, he was introduced to the supervisor in charge who shook his hand and escorted him over to the body. Lifting the plastic sheeting, he asked him if he could identify the body.

Looking down into the face of the now-lifeless man, he replied, "Yes, his name was Jason Stevenson, an ex-employee of Steven Chatsworth."

After replacing the sheeting they stepped aside and the supervisor said, "I also understand you're familiar with the remaining two we're searching for?"

"That is correct," he responded.

"Maxwell, frankly we don't know their identity, but you do. Would you mind going down to the station and meeting with our sketch artist?"

"No, I wouldn't mind at all."

"Thank you and welcome aboard. We can certainly use your expertise in this case. And yes, I know who you are," he said smiling. Maxwell returned the smile, and after speaking briefly with Skylar returned to his car and left the area.

While en route to the police station, he called Blake Colwell on his car phone and apprised him of everything including the deceased man's name. Blake said, "Brad, that means the other two are possibly still someplace in the surrounding area."

"Oh, I don't know about that, Blake."

"What do you mean? I sense a lot of uncertainty."

"Look at it this way: if you've just killed a man, would you stick around the area knowing the authorities are already searching for you?"

"No, I would not."

"That's precisely my point. Joker might be wild, Blake, but he's far from stupid. I don't know what happened to provoke the incident down there, but he's up to something, I'm certain of it. I'll be in touch." "Stay safe, buddy."

"Will do," he replied.

Maxwell walked up to the front desk at the Santa Monica Police Department. Upon giving his name, he was immediately escorted back to the sketch artist, who was a tall, slender green-eyed brunette with a captivating smile and large dimples carrying a large sketch pad. After introducing herself, she asked him to have a seat and the task began. Within an hour's time, there were faces on the two suspects. In his description of them were their weight, height, build and distinguishable marks that he'd noted on them. As he was leaving the station, Maxwell thought to himself, man, she's really good. Suddenly remembering Chatsworth's demeanor, he spoke out loud, "That old buzzard's too mean and ornery to die," musing to himself.

Within an hour's time, the duo's description was being distributed throughout the surrounding areas including television and the news media. Things were rapidly changing for the Santa Monica Police Department. Now they had a homicide case on their hands, but they also had the identity of the suspects, which wasn't available to them before. Since the victim was shot in the upper torso both front and back it was uncertain if more than one weapon was used in the shooting and meant waiting for the coroners and a ballistics report.

As he returned to the crime scene, the coroner's vehicle was leaving the area. Parking his car nearby, he searched for Skylar and after a few minutes, he spotted him having a conversation with two other men. They were also dressed in plain clothes and being familiar with policy he was certain they were the one's that had been assigned to take over the case. Skylar looked in his direction, smiled, excused himself from the two and walked over to Maxwell. " I see you made your way back, huh?"

"Yes, it took much less time than I'd anticipated. You know she's really good, Skylar."

"Yes, she is, and from the report I received you did a tremendous job in supplying the descriptions which will make it much easier for all of us." "Glad to have been of assistance," Maxwell spoke with a wide grin.

Skylar said, "Now it's just a matter of time before they're apprehended."

Maxwell gave him a steady gaze and said, "I'm not certain about that,

Skylar."

"Oh, oh, what are you thinking now, Maxwell?"

" I just have a gut feeling that Joker's up to something else; he hasn't accomplished whatever it is he's planned to do."

"Why do you believe there's something else?" Skylar asked him.

"All right, we have two shootings that he's been implicated in and one resulted in death. According to the housekeeper's statement, Chatsworth was told by one of them that he 'wanted everything that he owed him', am

I correct?"

"Yes, that's correct."

"As of this minute, no one has any concept of what he meant by that statement. The only thing of certainty is the fact that it appears

Chatsworth was shot as the result of whatever it might be."

"Yes, that's correct."

"And just what provoked the second shooting and why kill one of his men is also a mystery?"

"Maxwell, you know you're raising some valid questions and we don't have answers to any of them. I'd say this situation is getting pretty sticky."

"My point precisely! But I believe apprehending them is going to be the greatest challenge, Skylar."

"Why do you believe that?"

"Because he's wild, not stupid. He's going to take every precaution to prevent getting caught before he gets whatever it is he's after. And right now, no one has figured out just what that is." Giving Maxwell a long, hard gaze, he said, "Oh well, the case has been reassigned to someone else anyway. You saw those two men I was talking with?"

"Yes, I did, and if my guess is correct, they're the ones who will be handling the case since the status of it has changed."

"You're quite correct; they're with the homicide division." Maxwell smiled at him and said, "This is only a reminder of how quickly a situation can develop a new twist."

"Man, you said it. I only hope they're caught soon before we have another report that he's killed someone else."

"Amen to that!"

"Well, what are your plans now, Skylar?"

"First, I'm going to check in with my supervisor; I'll probably be assigned to another case."

"What about you, Maxwell? What are you going to do, or need I ask?"

"Now just what do you mean by that question, Skylar?"

"You have something up your sleeve, so to speak."

"He gave him a broad grin and said, "I think I'm going to do a little scouting around on my own and find out what I can come up with."

"That's precisely what I thought you were going to say."

"Oh, you did, did you?"

"Yes, and be careful; these guys are facing attempted murder and murder charges. They've gone this far, and who can say what they're going to do next?"

"Your point is well taken. If I do happen to come upon something, I'll give you a call." Shaking hands, Skylar said, "That's fair enough." They each turned and walked away in opposite directions.

Maxwell sat in his car for a few minutes, then taking a brief glance at his wristwatch decided to grab a bite to eat. He thought to himself, Joker's not sticking around after what he's done, and I've got a hunch he's about to put his plan into effect, but the question still remains the same: what and how will he go about implementing it?

In the meanwhile, Skylar had returned to the station. Since the suspects had been positively identified, he began to do a background search for any known criminal history and found nothing on the deceased victim nor Flint Bishop, not even a traffic violation. Freddy Sinclaire was a different story. Apparently, two years prior, he'd been charged in a felonious assault case. The report stated that the incident occurred as the result of a joke he'd played on someone incurring bodily injury. But for some strange reason, the case never made it to trial and the charge was dismissed based upon insufficient evidence and the victim had mysteriously disappeared from the city. There was no record of any family or relatives for either one. Since a composite drawing of the duo was being distributed the opportunity to move in and about the area unnoticed was becoming very slim. A dragnet was set up in and about the surrounding areas. It appeared that Maxwell's perception of the two were correct that they hadn't stuck around after the shooting, but had left the immediate area. However, at that time, the authorities weren't aware of this. Approximately four hours later, Joker's 1992 red mustang convertible was found abandoned just two blocks away from the crime scene on a side street. The information was radioed into the station by a unit patrol that happened to have been patrolling that area.

Maxwell had just gotten into his car when the phone rang. Looking at the display, he said, "Hello, Skylar, this is Maxwell. What have you learned?"

"How did you know?" He gave a hearty laugh and said, "Just a lucky guess."

"Yeah, like I believe that one," he said, laughing. Anyway, I did some background investigation on the deceased man and our two remaining suspects and guess what came up?" "Surprise me," he said.

"There's no police record on the victim or Flint Bishop anywhere, not even a traffic violation, but—"

He interrupted. "Joker has a record?"

"You said it, man!"

"And it appears you've been right about him all along."

"How's that?" He gave him all of the information that he'd obtained. Maxwell said, "Considering the source, I can't say that I'm at all surprised. But what does surprise me is why there was no follow-up on the case, especially since the alleged victim had mysteriously disappeared."

Skylar said, "Man, I have no answers for you there. Then he informed him that Joker's mustang was found abandoned just two blocks away from the crime scene."

"Which means they're undoubtedly on foot because I've never seen Bishop driving; he's always been a passenger," Maxwell told him.

"What do you think, Maxwell?"

"Number one, I didn't expect them to stick around after the shooting, and two, I'm trying to figure out why he shot the other fellow, and three,

I believe he's working on his next plan of action."

"Why do you say that?"

"Skylar, I don't know right now; let's just say it's a feeling I have about this whole thing. Something's wrong with this picture."

"Sometimes, a gut feeling is all we have to go on, but can often be correct," he said.

"Yes, I know." Pausing briefly, Skylar said, "You sound troubled; what is it?"

"There's something not right about this situation. Listen, I'm going to check something out; where can you be reached?"

He immediately gave him his desk number and the cellular phone number. "I'll be in touch," Maxwell told him as he replaced the phone. Sitting in the car analyzing the situation and recalling his conversation with Skylar regarding the two suspects, he was certain there was something they were overlooking, but what? Just what was the issue with Chatsworth and Joker resulting in him having been shot? His instincts led him to believe there was much more to the incident than the three having been fired.

They were now approximately three blocks away from where Joker had parked his car. As he and Bishop were darting in and out of alleyways in an effort to elude the authorities, Bishop asked him, "Joker, where are we headed now? You know the cops are going to be looking everywhere for us?" Without taking his eyes off their surroundings, he said, "Yeah, I know that, but we sure can't go back to my ride so we'll just have to get one somewhere."

"What'd you mean, 'get one'? From where and how?" Bishop nervously asked.

Joker abruptly halted, stared directly at Bishop, and said "Look, stupid, just what do you think I mean? We need a ride to get out of here pronto and nobody's going to up and give us one?" He saw the desperation in Joker's eyes and kept silent knowing all too well what that look meant, he sure didn't want to end up the same way Stevenson did. A few minutes later, they found themselves behind a service station. After cautiously scooping out the area, Joker looked at Bishop and said, "Come on, follow me, we've got us a ride." He was hesitant at first. Joker stared hard at him for an instant and asked, "Are you coming with me or not?" His rapid response was, "I'm coming, Joker."

As they were approaching from the side of the building, Bishop was nervously scanning the area and only saw two cars at the isles. There was no one in the first car and an old man was just getting into the second one. Before he actually realized what was happening, Joker snatched the man out of the car and abruptly pushed him to the ground while holding the gun to his head. He then yelled, "Hurry up and get in the car, stupid."

Bishop immediately did as he was told and found himself getting sick by the minute because he was afraid that Joker was going to shoot the old man. But instead, he started to laugh louder and louder as they sped out of the service station into traffic. A few minutes later, they were on the freeway, which wasn't even a full city block from the service station. Bishop's stomach was churning inside, but the way Joker was behaving, he didn't want him to go off on him! There was already an all-points bulletin out on the duo. Now the carjacking and assault with a deadly weapon would also be added to the list of other charges alleged against them. During that time of day, the traffic was relatively light allowing them an opportunity to leave the area rather rapidly.

After they were some distance away from the service station, Bishop stared at Joker and hesitantly asked, "Where are we going now? You know the cops are going to be looking for this car."

Joker looked over at him, laughed, and said, "Right now we're getting away from this area. I know of a place where they won't be looking for us."

Bishop was fully aware of the fact that Joker didn't like to be questioned, but he was becoming nervous and decided to ask him anyway. "Joker, just where is this place you're talking about?"

Without taking his eyes off the traffic he said, "We're going to Arleta. I have a cousin there, and besides, he owes me a favor anyway."

"But Joker, what if he's not there? Then what will we do?" Bishop questioned.

Joker replied resolutely, "If he's not home I'll know where to find him."

Bishop wanted to ask Joker just what was the beef between he and Chatsworth because it had been in his thoughts since the incident first occurred. He soon realized that it was best to leave well enough alone and not push him. Knowing first-hand what he was capable of doing, Bishop didn't want to be his next victim so he remained silent. As he continued driving, Joker would periodically look in his side and rearview mirrors for any sight of the police or highway patrol. He didn't want to draw any attention to them by making certain he remained within the speed limits.

After about an hour's drive on the coastal route, approximately three quarters of a mile up ahead of them, Joker spotted a highway patrol car halting traffic. Suddenly and without warning, he exclaimed, "Drats!" Narrowly missing a rear-end collision, he abruptly drove into the outer lane and took the first available exit off the freeway.

Startled by his unexpected actions, Bishop stared wide-eyed at him and asked, "Joker, what's wrong with you, man? You nearly caused an accident back there."

After a few silent minutes he looked over at Bishop and said, "I saw the highway patrol stopping traffic just ahead of us. We'll have to go another way now."

At this point, Bishop was becoming uneasy and asked him, "Do you know how to get to where we're going from this direction, Joker?" "Yeah, it's just going to take us a little longer than I planned," he said.

Bishop remained silent after Joker's statement, but his inner thoughts were quite active. What if he hadn't spotted the patrol car until it was too late to get off the freeway? Jeeps, why did I get tied up with this lunatic? I knew he was nuts; now I'm tied up in a murder rap and carjacking and just because I was with him, that makes me an accessory to the crimes. Oh God, I hope there's no more killing.

During this time, Joker was having thoughts of his own. John D. had better be home; if not, I'll know where to find him. We have got to get rid of this car; maybe that's why the cop was stopping traffic. All I can say is they were lucky I saw them first. By this time, they're going to have road blocks everywhere and I don't plan on getting caught.

Maxwell was on his way to check out a tip he'd received regarding the two suspects. Suddenly, the radio station announced there had been a recent carjacking incident by two already sought-after fugitives. "What in heaven's name are we going to do next?" he questioned himself. He immediately dialed Skylar's telephone desk number at the Santa Monica police station. "Hello, this is Detective Jacob Skylar."

"Skylar, this is Maxwell. I just heard the news bulletin of a carjacking on the radio."

"Yes, that's correct, Maxwell. It occurred at a service station near the westbound 101 freeway and according to the description given by the victim, it was definitely our two suspects."

"Was anyone injured?"

"No, thank God for that! The sixty-seven-year-old was just frightened half to death because he stated that he thought the one holding the gun to his head was going to shoot him."

"That would have been Joker," Maxwell stated.

Skylar said, "With everything we know about them so far, I'm inclined to agree with you."

"Listen, Skylar, I received a tip from a source and was on my way to check it out. Perhaps it will lead to some type of clue as to what those two might be up to. I'll be in touch with you later."

While driving, Maxwell's thoughts were of the duo and wondered to himself, just what are their plans now and where might they be headed? Wherever they're going, obviously transportation is necessary. His thoughts were interrupted by the ring on his car phone, and looking down at the display, he said, "Hello, Blake, what can I do for you?"

"And hello to you, Brad. I saw the news bulletin on a carjacking incident implicating those two suspects. Have they been positively identified as the ones responsible?"

"Blake, according to the description given the authorities by the victim, I'm afraid they're the same two."

Blake exclaimed, "Great Caesar's ghost! Brad, what are those lunatics going to do next?"

"It's difficult to say at this point. They're on the run from the authorities and becoming desperate. Blake, I've been doing some scooping around. No one's really saying anything, but I believe Chatsworth's getting shot far exceeds the speculation that it was the result of Joker having been fired."

"Oh, and why do you believe that, Brad?"

"Blake, my instincts are telling me there's more involved in this Chatsworth incident than an angry disgruntled ex-employee."

"And just what might that be, pray tell?"

"Number one, before the shooting occurred, the housekeeper stated that she heard the other man tell Chatsworth, 'I want everything that's mine now!' And from all indications, the odds are we're assuming that was Joker and it didn't sound as if he was just speaking of back payment. Number two, what had he promised Stevenson and Bishop that would have influenced them enough to follow him back to the residence?

Certainly, it couldn't have been just about that and why kill one of them."

After a brief silence, Blake said, "I honestly don't know, Brad, and you've raised some valid questions here. It appears that this incident with Chatsworth is deeper than what was first perceived."

"None of this is making any sense, Blake, something's missing here and I have a feeling when we locate the source of the situation the answers will be there because it revolves around Chatsworth himself."

"How and in what way, Brad?"

"Right now, I don't really know, but I'm going to ask Skylar to check on something for me."

"I gather you have something specific in mind," Blake asked.

"Yes, I do, and when I find something out, I'll give you a call. As of right now, I'm on my way to check something out, it just might lead to a clue as to where those two are going. I'll get back with you later, Blake."

"I appreciate that, Brad, please be careful."

Smiling, he responded, "As always."

"This is Detective Jacob Skylar."

"Skylar, this is Maxwell."

"Hello, Maxwell, and what do I owe the honor of this call?" he asked.

Speaking with a wide grin on his face, Maxwell said, "and hello to you, Skylar. Are you free to speak?"

There was a brief silence and Maxwell assumed he was checking out his surroundings for privacy. Then Skylar's voice returned. "What's up, Maxwell?"

"Listen, Skylar, I'm on my way to check something out and in the meanwhile, I need a favor."

"Name it!"

"See if you can locate the name of the attorney who represented Joker in that assault case and who paid his fee. Also, the name of the victim in the case who suddenly disappeared."

"I'll see what I can do, and I've a distinct feeling that you're on to something, Maxwell."

"Well, let's just say I'm following a hunch, Skylar, and see what develops in the process. I'll be in touch, and thanks for the help."

"You're welcome, Maxwell. Just keep me informed, will you?"

"You have my word, Skylar."

Approximately three hours later after the carjacking incident, Joker drove inside a mobile home park. Just beyond the entranceway, he spotted a pay telephone and after quickly looking around the area, he told Bishop to sit tight and keep his eyes open as he was getting out of the car. After a very brief conversation on the telephone, he returned and told Bishop, "We're in luck; he's home."

A few minutes later, they were pulling into a space that was occupied by a blue late model pickup truck that was parked beside a large mobile home. As they were getting out of the car, a man came out of the door and began walking towards them. As he approached, Bishop gasped and did a double take. Looking first at Joker, then at the other man, he said, "Good gracious, Joker, you two look like twins."

They both laughed heartily, and Bishop thought to himself, I wonder if he's as loony as Joker.

After hugging each other, Joker introduced Bishop to his cousin, John D., who acknowledged him with a smile saying, "I'm glad to meet you, Bishop." He hurriedly ushered them inside the house.

The three of them were sitting at the kitchen table sipping their cooler lights when John D. looked at Joker with a concerned expression on his face and asked, "How long are you two planning to stay? You know you've made headline news?"

For the first time, Bishop observed a seriousness about Joker he'd never seen before in his tone of voice and facial expression, as he looked directly at John D. and said, "Not long, man, just until tonight. I don't want to get you and Lizzie involved. By the way, where is she? I didn't see her car when we pulled in?"

"She's been in Santa Maria for a few days visiting her mother and she's coming back tomorrow. You know if she finds you here there's going to be the devil to pay."

Joker laughed and said, "Don't worry, we'll be long gone before she comes back." He stared deeply at John D. and said, "All I need is a little cash and a different ride; we've got to ditch this one pronto."

"Man, I hear what you're saying. I've only got about a hundred and fifty bucks here and you're welcome to it." Joker gave him a half-smile and said, "Thanks, cousin, you'll get it back."

John D. gave him a long stare and said, "I'm not worried about the dough I get paid in two days, but I am concerned about you. What are you planning to do?"

Joker stood up, pushed his chair back from the table, and walked over to the window, which was partially opened. Standing there with his back to them while peeking through the blinds and in a smooth and sullen tone he said, "John D., I think it's best that you don't know. If by some chance the cops happen to trace us here, there won't be anything you can tell them. And there's only one other person out there who knows about you and he's in the hospital."

Bishop, suddenly wide-eyed, stared into the face of the man sitting at the table across from him and as he turned his head, Joker was walking back towards them. Bishop saw an expression on his face that caused chills to run up his spine. As Joker was seating himself, Bishop wondered, how could Chatsworth have known about John D. and no one else did, because Joker certainly never mentioned anything about having a family. That is, until we were on our way here."

As he began to sip on his drink, John D. looked at Joker and asked him, "For my own peace of mind, just what did happen between you and the old man? The news is reporting that the authorities are looking for you as a suspect in the shooting at his home."

Bishop became nervous as Joker took a long sip from the bottle. Then, slowly and deliberately setting the bottle down on the table, gazed directly at John D. and said, "He had me do all of his dirty work and when it got too hot for him he fired me, can you believe that?"

John D. said, "Wait a minute, he can't fire you, you're not just someone who was working for him. Is that what the shooting was about?" In the meanwhile, as the two men spoke, Bishop was in a state of bewilderment and was slowly absorbing everything that was being said. It was late afternoon when he entered the bar on Crenshaw Boulevard. The stench of stale cigars, cigarette smoke and beer penetrated Maxwell's nostrils.

His inner thought was, how can people take this junk into their system and enjoy it? Oh well, to each his own.

Casually observing the surroundings, it definitely would not have been an environment of choice to take a date, even if he were to have one. He could sense the eyes of suspicion upon him by those that were not otherwise preoccupied with billiards or the pinball machines. As he approached the bar and chose a stool, a tall athletic-looking man with salt and pepper hair and deep-set dark penetrating eyes stared at him briefly,

then asked, "What'd you have to drink?"

Maxwell said, "I'll have a seltzer water if you don't mind."

The man looked at him and said, "A seltzer it is." He gave him the drink and asked if there was anything else.

Maxwell looked directly into his eyes and said, "Yes, as a matter of fact there is. I'm looking for a man called Big Mike."

The man eyed him for a full minute, then said, "You've found him; I'm Big Mike."

"My name is Bradford T. Maxwell; I'm a private investigator. Pete Sorenson said I should talk to you."

Staring at Maxwell with a puzzled expression, he asked him, "Talk to me about what?"

Taking a brief glance at each end of the bar, Maxwell refocused his attention back on Big Mike asking him, "Is there some place where we can have this conversation without an audience?"

With a steady gaze on Maxwell seeing the determined look in his eyes and his own curiosity, he said, "Yeah, and called a man named Jake, he told him to take charge of the bar for a while."

The man gave Maxwell a quick glance, then asked, "Is everything all right, boss?"

Shedding his white apron, Big Mike replied, "Yes, Jake, everything's fine."

To Maxwell, Jake looked as if he could afford to drop a hundred or so pounds, as Big Mike was leading them away from the bar and staring eyes. They walked approximately ten feet to the rear, then Big Mike abruptly stopped in front of a door with a black and gold embossed plaque that read private in bold letters. He reached into his trouser pocket, withdrew a small ring of keys after fingering through them, and finally selecting one, he unlocked the door and ushered Maxwell inside, closing the door behind them. He invited him to have a seat pointing to a small brown leather sofa that was positioned against the wall, which was desert sand in color. Near the center of the room was a medium-sized desk with a matching swivel chair and on the wall directly behind stood a six drawer metallic-colored file cabinet. Maxwell observed another door and assumed it might have been his private restroom.

Big Mike was the first to speak and asked, "Now, Maxwell, just what is it that you want to talk with me about?"

Looking directly at him, Maxwell replied, "I understand Joker and his buddies spent a great deal of their leisure time here."

Big Mike leaned forward placing both elbows on the desk interlacing his fingers, and in a rather stern tone said, "Maxwell, I hope the cops catch that psychopath real soon."

"Oh, and why do you say that, Big Mike? I get the impression that you don't particularly care for him."

"You've got that right; he's a boastful bully as well as a lunatic." "In what way?" Maxwell asked him.

Suddenly, as if he'd received a shock wave, Big Mike lowered his arms to the desk and gazing into Maxwell's eyes said, "Wait a minute;

you said you're a private investigator and Pete sent you here. There has to be a reason."

"My answer is yes on both counts," was Maxwell's reply. Then he said, "Big Mike, I'm investigating a case in which I strongly believe Joker is in some way tied into it. I'm trying to get some kind of information that will give an indication as to where he might be headed."

The man looked at him and said, "Maxwell, as long as it's away from my business, but just what is it that you want to know?"

"You stated earlier that he was a boastful bully. How was he boasting?"

"Oh, he'd beat the guys at the machines, then he'd tell them that he could buy the machines and pay them to work for him."

"I take it he's created a few problems here?" Big Mike gave him a hard stare and said, "That's putting it mildly."

"Oh, and in what way might I ask?"

"Well," he said as he began to lean back in the chair, "Joker first began coming here regularly a little over two years ago. He'd have a few beers and play billiards with the guys. But after a while, I guess it wasn't exciting enough for him because that's when he started playing pranks on them, and it seemed to have become a routine with him—"

At that point, Maxwell interrupted him by asking, "Why do you say that?"

"Every time he came, he'd always pull some idiotic prank on one of them before he left here. One night I had to break up a fight between he and another customer because he grabbed the guy's glass of beer and poured a full bottle of Red Rooster hot sauce in it. I told him then if he pulled one more prank he wouldn't be allowed back in here and told him to pay for the man's beer."

"What happened after that?" Maxwell asked him.

He laughed and said, "Oh, there was some reluctance, but he paid for it. He didn't come back for a couple of weeks, then one evening he came in, I was attending the bar, and when the regulars saw him, they all began to keep their distance."

Smiling, Maxwell asked, "Wouldn't you have done the same thing?"

"I certainly would have," he replied. There was a brief period of silence between them. Finally, Big Mike spoke and Maxwell became acutely aware of the change in his tone of voice as he said, "I shouldn't have allowed him to come back in here; that was my mistake."

"Hello, Kate, this is Jacob Skylar."

"Skylar, what a pleasant surprise. It's been quite a while. What have you been up to, or should I ask?"

He laughingly replied, "Yes, it has been a while. And to answer your question, I've been working as usual, but this time I want to ask a favor of you."

She laughed and said, "Yes, you're Jacob Skylar. In what way can I be of assistance to you this time? Nothing illegal, I hope?'

"Now, I wouldn't ask anything like that of you."

"Well, I should think not," she said smiling. On a more serious note, she asked him, "Just what is it you need, Jacob?"

"I'd like for you to pull up some information from the court files database, Kate. This is very important and urgently needed."

She was silent for a moment, then asked, "Skylar, what is the information that you need?"

He said, "Approximately two years ago there was a felonious assault case filed against a man named Freddy Sinclaire, but for some unknown reason the case never made it to trial. It appears that the victim suddenly disappeared just before that time. The charge against him was subsequently dismissed based upon insufficient evidence."

Kate abruptly asked, "Skylar, wait a minute, did you say Freddy Sinclaire?"

"Yes, Kate, I did."

Then she asked him, "Isn't he one of the guys the authorities are searching for in that Santa Monica murder case?"

"Yes, he's the same man," she said. "Skylar, that man has a very serious problem. How soon would you need this information?"

He said, "Doll, just as soon as you're able to get it," and gave her his cellular phone number.

Approximately two hours later, Skylar's cell phone rang. "Skylar, this is Kate. It took a little while, but I believe this is the information that you want."

He said, "Let's have it."

She immediately complied and said, "The attorney who represented Sinclaire was Victor Atkins—"

He quickly interrupted her. "What?! He was disbarred last year."

She said, "Oh, well, he was the attorney on the case at the time."

He asked her, "What's the next one?"

She replied, "A Mr. Steven Chatsworth put up the cash for his bail."

Skylar asked, "Are you certain?"

She said, "According to the records, yes."

He was silent for a time, then said, "Maxwell is not going to believe this."

"What?" she asked.

"Oh, I was just thinking out loud and thanks a mil, doll."

"You're quite welcome, and Jacob, next time let the call be for a dinner date."

He laughed and said, "It will be my pleasure, Kate."

Bishop stared at Joker, then John D., mentally questioning what he meant when he said Chatsworth couldn't fire him. He had no concept that the answer to his question was forthcoming and much more until Joker said, "No, John D., the shooting wasn't about his trying to fire me because he knew he couldn't. He told me to leave and don't come back; I didn't care about that, but I want everything that's mine and when I told him so, he refused. I went back for him to release my inheritance not with the intention to shoot him, but when he flatly told me to get out that's when I just lost it and shot him."

There was complete silence for a few minutes, then John D. said, "Man, I'm sorry it came to that, there should have been some way for you to reason with him; after all, he is your uncle." Suddenly, Bishop, who had been sitting silently by, quickly gulped a swallow of liquid and began to gag. John D. quickly gave him a couple of smacks on his back, then he was fine physically, but mentally he was coming loose at the end. Joker stared at his flushed face and burst into laughter, but to Bishop nothing at that point was amusing. Once recouped, he thought to himself, so that's why he was always trying to put Stevenson and me down, but he's the one who is nuts.

John D. said, "Cousin, you're lucky the old man's not dead and let's face it, he's your legal guardian; that's the way your folks had it set up. But what I can't understand is why he didn't release it to you last year when you turned twenty-five?"

"I was told that by chance if anything should ever happen to them he was to teach you the business and a sense of responsibility of how to use the money to establish a business of your own."

Joker stared at him awhile, then asked, "John D., who told you all this, because we only discussed it once and he said I should be patient, but a lot of his business I still don't know about."

A serious expression began to dawn on John D.'s face as he stood up, walked over to the refrigerator and brought three more bottles of coolers back to the table, giving Joker and Bishop theirs, then opened his. After taking a large sip, then slowly setting the bottle down and gazing directly at Joker, he said, "Freddy (that was the very first time Bishop had heard John D. call him by that name, and he was beginning to feel somewhat uneasy because he had no concept of what he was about to say) Uncle Jack told me it was about three months before they passed. He came here one evening after I had just gotten home from work and said he wanted to talk to me about something. I told him sure. We sat here at the table and this has gone through my mind many times since. It was as if he already knew something was going to happen because he said, 'John D., you're a few years older than Freddy and more stable. If I was to talk to him about the decision his mother and I've made regarding his welfare well, I'm afraid he wouldn't understand because he's still somewhat wild and irresponsible to him;

everything's a joke. We've discussed this with Steven and taken care of the necessary formalities. If by chance anything should happen to us, he's to be Freddy's legal guardian until age twenty-five. We've agreed that he's to teach him about the business, and hopefully, he will also learn what it means to be responsible. After he's learned these things, he's to use the money and assist him in acquiring a lucrative business of his own. I suppose we could have done it another way, but his mother and I both agree that perhaps Steven is our best option. He's much older and already well established in his profession and aside from that, he's her only brother'."

Suddenly, Joker slammed the bottle down on the table and Bishop instantly jumped back because he'd seen him in that state before, but amazingly enough, John D. never quenched, just maintained his gaze on him. Joker asked, "Why did they choose him? For as long as I can remember he's always been a stickler for perfection."

John D. stared at him for a minute or so before speaking. "Cousin, you're probably not going to like what I'm about to say, but I'll tell you anyway. I don't think anyone else wanted the responsibility of having to deal with you. You were spoiled and as the result, they were always bailing you out of one incident after another because you pulled those stupid pranks on people and laughed it off as a joke.

Bishop thought to himself, so that's why he's called Joker.

"But no one was ever seriously hurt," Joker retorted.

This time, John D. spoke in a much different tone. In fact, it was rather stern when he said, "Look, it's time for you to grow up and assume responsibility for your own actions. Has it ever occurred to you that just

maybe the old man feels you're not ready yet?"

Joker yelled, "But it's my money."

"Yes, that's true, but there was an agreement between he and your parents and he's abiding by their wishes; that's the only way I can figure it out."

Joker gave him a steady gaze and asked, "Just what am I supposed to do in the meantime, John D., since you seem to have all of the answers?"

"You're wrong about that, cousin. I don't have all the answers, but this much I do know: you're in a lot of trouble right now and the only one who can straighten it out is you and for once in your life, think about it!"

Little did John D. realize that while he was talking, Joker was thinking, but his thoughts were of how to get transportation for he and Bishop out of there and fast.

Maxwell gazed steadily at Big Mike and said, "From what you've said, I get the impression that you regret having allowed Joker back into the bar, and in what way do you feel it was a mistake if I might ask?"

Big Mike stared hard at him and said, "Maxwell, when he came in that time, a man was seriously injured. He ended up in the hospital and Joker went to jail."

Maxwell asked, "What happened here for him to have been arrested?"

"I was busy taking care of customers and didn't see the incident when it first occurred. Jake saw it all because he was collecting the bottles and glasses at the time. From what I was told, Joker and one of the newer customers got into an argument over one of the pinball machines. Joker started laughing and before he could break it up, he snatched up a bottle of beer, hitting the kid and breaking his jaw. By that time, the music had stopped, and I could hear Joker swearing, telling Jake to take his hands off him. After I saw what had actually happened, I called an ambulance and the police. They handcuffed him and took him out as he yelled, 'I'll be out! You're not going to keep me locked up!'"

"And just what do you suppose he meant by that?" Maxwell asked him. Big Mike leaned back in his chair and said, "I really can't say for sure.

Maybe he does have the money that he was boasting about."

Slowly gazing at him, Maxwell asked, "How do you figure that?"

Big Mike said, "Well, he or someone else does, because according to the rumor that was going on around here at the time, his bail was set pretty high and two days later he was back on the streets, but he never came back here."

There was complete silence for a few minutes, then Maxwell asked,

"Are you able to recall when all of this transpired?" He said, "Yes, it was two years ago, this month."

"Oh, why are you so certain?"

He stared directly at him and said, "Because that was the day my ex-wife had me served with divorce papers after twenty years of marriage." Maxwell said, "Man, I'm sorry to hear that."

"Oh well, she got what she wanted, and I still have this place." He was silent for a brief time, then said, "Maxwell, there's something I never quite understood about the whole incident with Joker." "What is that?" he asked of him.

"A number of things. For one, I understand he was charged with felonious assault. Number two, before he was to go to trial, the victim just happened to have mysteriously disappeared so it was rumored, and for about two weeks or more after that the detectives came around asking if anyone had seen the fellow or knew where he might be. I'll tell you something; all of that seems rather strange to me."

Maxwell leaned back, crossed his legs and said, "You've got a point there; it does appear to be odd considering the charge alleged against him. Did you ever hear Joker mention any relatives that he might have?"

Big Mike thought for a few seconds and replied, "No, none that I can recall."

Maxwell uncrossed his legs, stood up, and smiling, said, "Thank you for taking the time to have this conversation with me; I appreciate it."

At that point, Big Mike also stood up, walked around the desk, and said, "You're welcome. I'm sorry that I couldn't have been of more help to you. I hope they catch those two soon though."

"So do I, Big Mike," he responded. After shaking hands and walking through the door, Big Mike said, "Hey, Maxwell, the next time you're this way, the seltzer is on me."

"Thanks, I'll be sure to remember that" he said as he was leaving out of the door.

He had just started the engine when the car phone rang, and looking at the display, he said, "Hello, Skylar, this is Maxwell. Were you successful in learning anything?"

"I certainly was and Maxwell, you're not going to believe this."

"Then surprise me. Let's see what you've managed to come up with."

"The attorney who represented Joker in the assault case was none other than Victor Atkins—"

Maxwell interrupted him with, "You don't say! Wasn't he disbarred from practicing law after having been indicted by a grand jury for illegal practices and obstruction of justice?"

"Yes, he was, but that came after he'd represented Joker. In fact, it was last year."

"I don't suppose you have an address for him available?" he asked laughing.

"As a matter of fact, I do." Skylar gave him the attorney's telephone number and address.

Then Maxwell asked him, "What's next on your list?"

"Steven Chatsworth put up the bail money."

"Oh, he did, did he?"

"Yes, according to the information that I received."

"Skylar, if Chatsworth put up the cash for Joker's bail, then why would he fire him, and who paid Atkins to represent him? From what I've heard, his services don't come cheap."

"You've got a point there. Maxwell, perhaps you might be able to get some answers from Atkins himself. You can be quite persuasive, you know?"

"Only when necessary, Skylar." Then he said, "Something has just occurred to me."

Skylar promptly asked, "And what is that?"

"Something's fishy here. What if the victim was paid a large sum of money by someone to suddenly disappear from the scene before the trial date?"

"Well, what you're suggesting is plausible, but if proven as you well know, that's called obstruction of justice also; it's been known to happen."

"Who would be going to such great lengths just to keep Joker out of prison, and what could possibly be the motive behind it,?" Skylar asked him.

Maxwell said, "There it is again."

Bewildered by his statement, Skylar asked, "Maxwell, what do you mean?"

He quickly replied, "Skylar, this is the third time that the word, 'motive', has been applied in this situation. The first time is when Chatsworth was wounded. The second time was the Stevenson shooting, and now Joker's case."

Skylar asked him, "What are you thinking now, Maxwell?"

"Skylar, at this point I'm thinking that Chatsworth is somehow involved in this thing much deeper than what has been speculated."

"Why do you believe that?"

"Because each time we strike with Joker, haven't you noticed that Steven Chatsworth's name comes up?"

"Well, I'll grant you this, it is a baffling situation and all I can say is go with your instincts, pal."

"I'm not quite certain how the two of them are tied into this together just yet. Let's see what Atkins has to say and thanks, Skylar, I'll be in touch."

After the conversation with Detective Skylar concluded, Maxwell decided it would be more appropriate if he telephoned Attorney Atkins first, but what he really wanted to learn was whether or not he'd be cooperative by agreeing to meet with him. The telephone conversation between them was quite brief and successful because the attorney did agree to meet with him.

It was early afternoon when Maxwell and Atkins met at a quaint little coffee shop on Palo Verdes Boulevard. It was located in a somewhat elegant shopping center surrounded by a number of three-story office buildings that had been recommended by Atkins himself. Maxwell had barely gotten out of his car when Atkins pulled up beside him and parked. As he was getting out of his car, Maxwell was closely observing a man who appeared to be in his mid-sixties with greying hair, of medium height and a stocky statue. Maxwell thought he might be meeting someone dressed in a suit and tie, but instead he was casually dressed in a light-blue cardigan sweater, white shirt and blue trousers.

After a brief observation of the now-filled-to-capacity parking lot and seeing no one else, he turned to Maxwell and said, "You're Bradford T. Maxwell, I presume."

Maxwell gazed at him, smiled and said, "Your presumption is correct and I believe you're Attorney Atkins."

With deep-set grey penetrating eyes and thick eyebrows raising one upward slightly, he smiled while extending his hand out to Maxwell and said, "Yes, I'm Victor Atkins."

They turned and walked inside the coffee shop. There appeared to be only two unoccupied booths remaining and Maxwell chose the one with his back against the wall and immediately took occupancy in that seat. He preferred to face the entrance. Atkins didn't appear to mind. However, he did mentally take note of Maxwell's sitting position, smiled to himself, and thought, a very cautious man who doesn't easily present his back.

He quickly sat down in the opposite seat. There were only four booths, two tables and the counter. Nearly every seat in the shop was occupied. A short while after seating themselves, a young redheaded waitress with a pleasant smile asked if they were ready to order. They each ordered club sandwiches on rye and coffee. Maxwell also ordered a slice of apple pie topped with a scoop of vanilla ice cream.

While awaiting their orders, Atkins focused his eyes directly on him and said, "Maxwell, I agreed to meet with you for two reasons."

Slightly leaning back in the booth, he asked, "Oh, is that a fact?"

Atkins replied, "Yes, it is."

Maxwell stared at him and smiling asked, "And just what are your two reasons if I might ask?"

Their orders arrived and they both remained silent until the waitress had left their table. Then Atkins said, "Number one, for the moment let's just say I'm rather curious to learn why a private investigator such as yourself would be interested in talking with me. And number two, I'm no longer permitted by law to practice my profession, as I'm quite certain you're aware of." With his eyes slightly squinted and smiling, Maxwell gazed at him and asked, "Just how do you mean, such as myself?" "Oh, come now, Maxwell, you don't have to be so modest." "I fail to see the point of inference, Atkins," he responded.

"Certainly, you don't believe I would agree to talk with someone before learning something about them first, do you?"

"I get your point, but you can't believe everything that you hear."

"That's true, but after meeting you, Maxwell, in this case I must admit your reputation is no mystery and I'm also aware of the fact that you're the one who investigated the Lansing contractors' firm scandal. And was quite successful in bringing a resolve."

"See, Atkins, this is precisely what I meant by you can't believe everything that you hear."

"I don't understand, Maxwell."

"What you've stated is correct in part."

"What do you mean correct in part?"

He took a sip of coffee, leaned back, and while never taking his eyes off him said, "Atkins, I don't know what you've heard, but the fact of the matter is the case hasn't been completely resolved. That is, not yet anyway. You see there are still some loose ends that have to be tied up before there can be a resolve. Oh, we know who's responsible for creating the situation and why, but it's more complicated than that, I can assure you."

Atkins gazed at him and said, "I'm not following you."

Maxwell stared hard into the man's eyes and said, "About two years ago, you represented a man who had been charged with felonious assault; his name was Freddy Sinclaire. Does that ring a bell?"

"Yes, I remember handling the case, but why do you ask?"

"I'll answer your question after you've answered the two, I'm going to ask you."

"Just what are these two questions, Maxwell?"

"It's a known fact that your services didn't come cheap. So, what I'd appreciate hearing from you is this: who hired you to represent Sinclaire and paid his attorney's fee?"

"Maxwell, why is that so important to you because it certainly appears to be?"

"Listen, Atkins, you haven't answered my question and don't give me that bunk about attorney and client's privilege because it doesn't apply in this case." At that point he knew Atkins was hedging and he was interested in learning why. Therefore, he decided to go farther. "Atkins, let's stop playing the cat-and-mouse game here and get down to serious business."

He retorted, "I don't know what ever you mean."

"All right, since you're determined to have it this way, I'm going to lay it out for you."

"By all means, Maxwell, please do."

"Your former client was charged with felonious assault on another human being that resulted in serious injury requiring hospitalization. His bail was set at such an exuberant amount that only someone with a lot of money could afford to pay. Sinclaire was never known to posses such wealth, and he certainly didn't earn that kind of money working for Chatsworth. Atkins, you know what strikes me as being odd? The case never made it to trial because just before the trial date, the victim suddenly and mysteriously disappeared and was never seen again."

There was a brief period of silence and Maxwell was thinking to himself, he's concealing something, and I'll bet he's trying to make a decision as to how he should respond.

It appeared that his perspective of Atkins was correct. Because he took a long sip of coffee and after slowly setting the cup down, he said, "Continue on, Maxwell."

"There's another fact that can be seen here. The case was dismissed based on insufficient evidence and I certainly would consider that to be of a suspicious nature. Now the same man is being sought by the authorities for murder and attempted murder, on his former ex-employer Steven Chatsworth and so far, no one has been able to come up with a motive as to why. However, I'm certain of one thing: the shooting of Chatsworth had nothing to do with Sinclaire's termination. I believe there's much more involved here than just a disgruntled ex-employee."

Staring at him, Atkins asked, "Why do you believe that Maxwell, because it's a reality that these are occurring incidents whether we like it or not."

"Yes, that's correct and it's sad, but Sinclaire's case is different; he's after accomplishing something that is important to him." Maxwell planned to maintain his leverage by not divulging the information he'd already obtained prior to their meeting.

Atkins remained silent. He just leaned back, letting his head rest on the booth. But his gaze on Maxwell never altered who incidentally didn't mind the waiting period. Besides, he was enjoying his dessert with the satisfaction of knowing that he'd given Atkins just enough ammunition for him to discharge. Maxwell began to observe an expression of sadness appear upon Atkins's face and wondered why the abrupt change. At that same moment, the answer to his question was about to be revealed. He learned that Atkins had once been part of a lucrative law firm a short distance from where they were prior to being disbarred. Maxwell had a feeling there was more to the story, but he didn't press the matter.

Atkins stared out of the window for a couple of minutes, then turned his gaze upon him and said, "Maxwell, I was Steven Chatsworth's attorney, had been for years. He put up the money for Sinclaire's bail and also paid me to represent him in the case you spoke of. Of course, I advised him against it, but that was the way he wanted it."

Maxwell said, "Wait a minute, Atkins, you're losing me. Why would Steven Chatsworth put out that kind of money for a lunatic like Joker?" He was certain that Chatsworth had played an integral role in Sinclaire's case. He was interested in learning how. The answers could not come from Chatsworth himself; but Atkins was definitely in a position to oblige him with the information he was seeking. Maxwell had no concept that the answers to both questions were forthcoming and much more than he would ever have imagined.

"Joker, how long do you think it'll be before the cops find the car?" Bishop asked him.

He stared over at him and said, "I would imagine when they open the place up for business in the morning."

Bishop was silent for a while, then said, "I sure wish we could've found a different kind of transportation to get back, because we're going to be smelling just like these chickens."

Apparently, Joker was becoming annoyed because he snarled at Bishop and said, "I figured this would be the best way to travel. The cops are not going to be looking for us in the back of a truck loaded with live poultry. So, stop your whimpering, will you?"

"I'm just glad we left before John D.'s old lady got there. She might've called the cops on us. She never had much liking for me anyway." "Yeah, me too," Bishop agreed.

Joker had paid the driver of the truck fifty dollars to let them ride in the back of the truck. John D. knew the man, so he took the money without question while thinking to himself if they want to smell like a poultry farm that's their business. Joker still had the gun and Bishop was silently praying that they wouldn't be stopped, and the truck searched by the cops. He was fed up with all of the shooting, but kept his concerns to himself, knowing quite well that if he expressed his feelings Joker would be all over him in a minute. He was already agitated anyway, but he wasn't responsible for the predicament they were in.

Suddenly, the truck began to slow down, then came to a complete halt. Joker stared at Bishop, who at that instant was also staring at him wide-eyed. They were each aware of what was happening; they'd encountered a roadblock.

Bishop was praying silently, Lord, please don't let them find us, I don't want to see any more bloodshed.

Joker had taken his gun out and was pointing it directly at the truck's large door. What seemingly had been a long few minutes they heard voices outside, then the truck began to move again and Bishop gave a deep sigh of relief saying, "Thank you, Lord." Joker never uttered a word, just returned the gun to its place of concealment.

Maxwell gazed at Atkins steadily and said, "You stated that you advised Chatsworth against paying out the money for Sinclaire's bail and defense; why was that?"

"I personally felt that he should have faced the consequences for his actions by assuming responsibility for the crime he committed." "Wouldn't that have been a conflict of interest on your part?"

"Oh, I would have recommended someone, shall we say, with less experience in criminal strategy. It happens more frequently than most people realize, Maxwell."

"So, you defended him anyway in spite of your reservations?"

"Yes, I did, because not only was I Steven's attorney, I'm also his friend and I felt he was making a terrible mistake."

"You have yet to answer my question as to why, and don't tell me it was out of the kindness of his heart."

Atkins cleared his throat and said, "I believe I can say just that, Maxwell. You see, with Steven it was the matter of making a personal choice."

At that point, Maxwell was beginning to grow weary of Atkins's hedging. Tt was time to change tactics. Maxwell gave him a stern look and asked, "What do you mean it was the matter of making a personal choice, Atkins? How is it personal, and I prefer to hear all of it?" Before allowing him to answer, Maxwell decided to sprinkle more cinnamon on Atkin's toast. Sitting upright, moving the dessert dish aside and staring directly into his eyes he said, "Atkins, the lunatic you reluctantly defended regardless of your personal motive is the same one who is responsible for the condition Chatsworth is in. I'm not quite certain right now what it is, but my gut is telling me that he's planning something else."

The man gazed hard at him and asked, "Why do you believe he's planning something else when the authorities are searching every place for him, Maxwell?"

"For one thing, he's wild, not stupid. He could very easily have killed Chatsworth, but he seriously wounded him instead, which left me to believe he wasn't thinking rationally and for some unknown reason, he lost self-control. Now, I'm curious to know why."

"Maxwell, I'm afraid I can't answer that question; I don't know if anyone can except Sinclaire himself."

"And Chatsworth, but he's in the hospital and no visitors are allowed as of right now," Maxwell interjected. During a brief period of silence, Maxwell observed Atkins staring what appeared to be blankly into space.

Suddenly, and to his astonishment, Atkins focused his eyes directly on him and said, "Maxwell, I've been sitting here listening to your scenario and thinking. Enough injustice has been done and I'm growing weary of it all. Mind you, no actual facts have been found to substantiate this, but what if your assumption is correct that Sinclaire is planning something and as right now, no one has any concept of what it might be?"

Leaning back in the booth and folding his arms across his broad chest, Maxwell said, "Go on, I'm listening."

"Considering Sinclaire's state of mind, whatever that is and the possibilities, I now feel compelled to answer your question regarding Chatsworth's personal choice. To begin with, Freddy Sinclaire is Steven Chatsworth's nephew."

At that revelation, Maxwell sat straight up and staring directly at Atkins exclaimed, "What!"

"That is correct; Freddy is Steven's nephew and there's more to follow. I'm only conveying this to you because I'm concerned for Steven's well-being and perhaps it will be of some use to you in determining what Freddy might be planning to do. When I represented Freddy the bail money was taken out of his trust fund. You see, Steven is Freddy's legal guardian until the age of twenty-five, or at his discretion after that. His mother was Steven's older sister. She and her husband were killed in an accident when Freddy was in his late teens, but prior to their deaths they had everything taken care of. Of course, Freddy didn't learn of the guardianship until much later."

Staring at him, Maxwell asked, "You mean to tell me that Sinclaire has that kind of money?"

"Yes, I'm afraid he has."

Maxwell asked, "What I find difficult to comprehend is why would he keep the relationship a secret, and why the pretext of firing him along with the others?" Staring at him curiously, he asked, "When was this, Maxwell?"

"Just prior to the shooting, he told them to get out of his sight and stay out."

Atkins gave him a puzzled look and asked, "How do you know this?" Maxwell said, "I was there."

With a bewildered expression on his face, Atkins asked him, "Where did this take place?"

"At his residence," he replied.

With apparent astonishment upon hearing the answer, he gazed hard at him for a brief instant, then asked, "You went to Seven Chatsworth's residence without having been invited?"

"Yes, I did, because what I had to tell him there was no rationale to feel I needed an invitation." At that, and seeing the expression on Atkins's face, Maxwell could only imagine what he might have been thinking but made no reference to the matter. He continued, "I went there to inform Chatsworth that I had notified the authorities regarding the despicable acts of his employees. After hearing what I had to say, he told them that they had disobeyed his orders and as far as he was concerned, the authorities could have the three of them."

Atkins looked away, then back again at him, and said, "The only explanation I can possibly think of is Chatsworth didn't want the others to know he's Freddy's uncle. I can't give you an answer as to why he preferred to have it that way. Steven Chatsworth is a very complicated and sometimes difficult man to understand and I never questioned his rationale for it."

Maxwell asked, "Does Sinclaire have siblings?"

"No, he was an only child and from what I've come to learn and see, he's been spoiled rotten. I believe Chatsworth was their last recourse."

"In reference to your statement regarding Sinclaire's age, which I believe was twenty-five, or at his uncle's discretion, what did you mean by that?"

Taking a deep sigh and leaning back in the booth with a steady gaze on him he said, "Maxwell, there was a verbal agreement between Freddy's parents and his uncle."

"And just what was that agreement, might I ask?"

"Well, Steven was to teach him the business and a sense of responsibility of how to use the money they'd left him to become established in a lucrative business of his own. But from what I've seen, he's still being irresponsible and I'm quite certain this is why the money is still being held in trust because he reached age twenty-five last year."

Maxwell was mentally assessing what he was being told, then asked himself, could this possibly be the motive for the shooting? He asked Atkins, "As to your knowledge, has Sinclaire asked Chatsworth for the money?"

"Yes, as a matter of fact, he has. Why do you ask?"

"This is what I'm trying to learn from you. What was Chatsworth's response when he asked for the money? Steven told him that he wasn't going to get a cent until he'd proven to him that he was sincere in learning the business and willing to assume responsibility of ownership. Oh, he became angry and belligerent, but that was the extent of it."

Maxwell said, "I'm not quite so certain of that."

Atkins stared at him and asked, "Why? What do you mean?"

Maxwell said, "Atkins, we've searched for a motive that would somehow explain Sinclaire's state of mind at the time of the shooting and I believe you just gave it."

"Wait a minute, Maxwell, are you implying that Freddy shot Steven because he refused to give him the money?"

"Yes, I'm implying just that. Can you think of any other motivating force that can explain his wild, irrational behavior?"

"No, I'm afraid I can't, Maxwell. I'd say overall there's a strong possibility that your perception is correct."

"Since they're on the run from the authorities, have you any concept where they might go?" Maxwell asked him.

Atkins said, "No, I'm afraid I haven't, and I'm certain no one around here is going to get involved with them."

Maxwell said, "Perhaps you're correct. But wherever they are, I have a hunch he's planning something."

"What, Maxwell, considering Chatsworth is still hospitalized?"

"Atkins, I don't know, it's difficult to say as of now. We have an irrational man who's completely out of control." Looking at his wristwatch and noting the time, he gazed at Atkins, smiled and said, "This has been a most rewarding afternoon. You've filled in the missing pieces to this end of the puzzle and I appreciate your cooperation, Atkins. Thank you."

He stared hard into Maxwell's eyes, smiled and said, "It's been quite some time since I've had the opportunity to spend such an enjoyable afternoon in the company of a man who's professional and tactful. I'm pleased with the outcome of this meeting, Maxwell, and to have met you."

Maxwell gave him a wide smile and said, "The feeling is mutual,

Atkins, I'll be in touch."

"I'd like that very much, Maxwell," he responded smiling.

Maxwell was en route to his office when the car phone rang and taking a quick glance at the display said, "Hello, Skylar. What are you up to this time—laughing heartily?"

"And hello to you, Maxwell. You recall the carjacking incident by our two fugitives. Well, we've just received information that the vehicle was found abandoned at a car wash up in Arleta. It appears that the owner found it parked there as he went to open up and reported it to the police who ran the plates and immediately called us."

"Well, well, it appears they've been doing some moving, wouldn't you say?"

Skylar laughed and said, "Yes, I would, Maxwell."

Following a brief pause, Maxwell asked him, "When did the station receive this call from the Arleta Police?"

Skylar said, "I believe it was around eleven-thirty this morning."

"Most car washes open up early in the morning for business, don't they?" Maxwell asked him.

"Yes, I believe they do, but why do you ask?"

"Skylar, if you were being sought after by the authorities and knew the car you're driving is hot, what and where would you consider to be the best time and place to get rid of it?"

He thought for a minute and said, "I see where you're coming from. Naturally, I'd wait until it's dark and no one's around to see me. Then I would make certain it'd be someplace where it wouldn't be discovered until the next day and by that time, I'd be long gone to wherever that might be."

"My point precisely," Maxwell responded.

Skylar said, "The authorities are doing their own investigation up there since the car was found in their jurisdiction. We'll just have to wait and see what they come up with, anything at all."

Maxwell laughed and asked, "What's the matter, Skylar? I sense a note of skepticism."

"I just don't think they will succeed in producing anything, Maxwell, and those two certainly wouldn't stick around after ditching the car. I'm very much interested in learning where they went after that and how."

"Now you're raising some valid questions, Skylar. Wherever they're headed has been under the cloak of darkness. There's less noticeable traffic and there's one thing for certain—they're still on the run and are somehow managing to elude the authorities."

Skylar asked, "Oh, by the way, Maxwell, how did your meeting with Atkins go?"

Suddenly, something hit him like a lightning bolt and he said, "Listen, Skylar, I'm en route back to my office. Something just occurred to me when you were asking about the meeting with Atkins. Are you going to be available within the next hour?"

Skylar replied, "Yes, I'm on evenings this week. What is it, Maxwell?"

"We just might have a break in this situation after all, Skylar. I'll be in touch."

After terminating the telephone conversation with Skylar, Maxwell arrived at his office a short time later and immediately began to mentally focus on the conversation he and Atkins had earlier.

Thinking out loud, he said, "This situation with Chatsworth and Joker has more twists and turns than a spinning top. As for Chatsworth, I find him quite a strange and unpredictable man, to say the least. Now I wonder just how long had he planned to keep the relationship a secret and what is the point of it anyway? He allowed everyone with the exception of one, Atkins, to believe Joker was just another employee, yet when he said they were all terminated Joker was the only one of the three who retaliated. Was that because he knew something that the others didn't? Atkins stated that he's Joker's legal guardian over the trust and he'd refused to give him the money when he asked for it. Now I suspect that is why Joker went back to the residence and if that's the case, his motive for shooting Chatsworth would have been the money. There's no logical explanation for his having gone off the deep end."

As Maxwell was mentally compiling all of the information into stages, the telephone on his desk began to ring, and looking at the caller ID he said, "Hello, Blake, I wasn't aware that you have ESP."

Blake responded, "Hello to you, Brad, and what is this about ESP?"

"Well, old buddy, it's as if you were reading my thoughts because I was just about to call you."

Blake chuckled and said, "Oh, I see. Well, what have you learned regarding the Chatsworth situation?"

Maxwell gave a hearty laugh, asking Blake, "Are you sitting down comfortably?"

There was a brief silence and Blake replied, "I am now and from the tone in your voice, I expect whatever it is that you're about to tell me is going to be interesting."

"Blake, I believe what I'm about to bring you up-to-date on you're going to find somewhat more than interesting." "Oh. Oh, please continue Brad," he said.

"I've been following up on a lead that had supplied me with information regarding Joker, as it turned out I met with Victor Atkins—"

On that note, Blake immediately interrupted him and asked, "Victor Atkins was disbarred, Brad. What does he have to do with Joker?"

"Blake, I hope you're ready for this," Maxwell said. "Approximately two years ago, Joker was charged with felonious assault against another young man in a bar fight. But the case never made trial because the victim mysteriously and suddenly disappeared prior to the trial date as a result, the charge against him was subsequently dismissed based upon insufficient evidence."

Blake exclaimed, "What?! That sounds rather suspicious to me, and no one ever followed up on the case?"

Maxwell said, "My sentiments exactly, but that is only a part of it.

Guess who the attorney handling his case was."

"Not Victor Atkins," Blake said.

"One and the same," Maxwell replied.

"Wait a minute, Brad, Victor Atkins was considered by some to have been a shrewd attorney who didn't come cheap. So, working for Steven Chatsworth, how in heaven's name could Joker have afforded his services?"

Maxwell said, "He couldn't, but Steven Chatsworth could and did. I didn't push Atkins into admitting Chatsworth also paid the victim to disappear and I'm certain he did because that would be his style of operating which meant he was guilty of obstruction of justice. Besides, I was more interested in learning how and why Chatsworth was involved in Joker's case, to begin with."

Blake said, "So am I, Brad."

Maxwell continued, "According to Atkins, Steven Chatsworth is Freddy Sinclaire's uncle and legal guardian."

Up until that time, Blake Colwell had been leaning back comfortably in his chair, but when he heard what Maxwell had just conveyed, he sat upright and asked, "Did I hear you correctly, Brad?"

He replied, "Yes, you did, Blake, Chatsworth is Joker's uncle. His mother was Chatsworth's older sister. According to Atkins, he was an only child and they'd left a substantial trust fund for him."

Blake asked, "Brad what I'd like to know is why on earth would he keep the relationship a secret?"

Maxwell laughed and said, "Blake, I asked Atkins that question and his answer was, and I quote, 'Steven Chatsworth is a very complicated and difficult man to understand. He wanted it that way and I certainly didn't question his rationale for it, unquote."

"Blake, we're seeking a motive for the Chatsworth shooting and I believe we have one," he said.

Blake said, "I don't understand, Brad."

"Atkins stated that the money for Joker is being held in a trust fund until age twenty-five; he's now twenty-six and still hasn't received it. I asked Atkins as far as he was aware of, had Joker asked Chatsworth for the money and his reply was yes. I asked him what Chatsworth's response was, 'Just what was his response when Joker asked him Brad?'"

"Again, according to Atkins, Chatsworth told him that he wasn't going to get a cent until he'd proven to him that he was serious about learning the business and willing to assume the responsibility of ownership. Apparently, his parents and Chatsworth had a verbal agreement pertaining to the trust."

Blake sighed and said, "When you informed me that the information was going to be interesting, I'd say that was an understatement."

"You know, Blake, everyone else has been speculating about a motive for the shooting, but I'll bet you a ten-dollar gold piece Chatsworth knows the answer."

"From everything you've conveyed to me, I'm inclined to agree with you, Brad," he said. "Incidentally, have you spoken with Detective Skylar recently?"

Maxwell's reply was, "Yes, earlier. As a matter of fact, I'm going to give him a ring next. It appears that the Arleta Police Department notified them, that the car taken by the two in the carjacking incident was found abandoned at a car wash there."

"In Arleta, what in heaven's name were they doing there, Brad?" Blake asked.

Maxwell said, "I haven't the vaguest concept Blake other than the fact that perhaps he's trying to throw everyone off track."

"Wait a minute, you mean like they're planning to do something else?" Blake asked.

"My instincts are telling me yes, they are, but at this point, I have no concept of what it is and it's annoying me to the utmost," he said.

"Listen, Blake, I'm going to give Skylar a call. I'll be in touch," he said.

"All right, Brad, just be safe."

He laughed and said, "I'll do my best, buddy."

"Hello, Skylar, this is Maxwell, can you spare a few minutes?"

The voice on the other end said, "Hold on a sec. Hello, Maxwell, sorry about that, but I had to switch phones and yes, I'm free for the moment," he replied.

He came right to the point and said, "Skylar, without going into all of the specifics right now, I believe we finally have a motive for the Chatsworth shooting incident."

There was a brief silence, then Skylar asked, "Are you certain, Maxwell?"

His direct response was, "I'm quite certain, Skylar, money was the motive. Do you recall asking me earlier how the meeting with Atkins went?"

"Yes, and I remember your abrupt response was something had occurred to you when I asked."

He said, "Yes, and I do apologize for that. Skylar, I would say the meeting was quite productive."

"Oh, really, just how productive, Maxwell?" he asked.

"Let's just say I learned a number of things that weren't on the scoreboard before. The information that you were successful in obtaining gave me the leverage I needed to, shall we say, bolt Atkins down. We've been searching in all of the wrong places for answers to this dilemma. Listen to this—Steven Chatsworth is Freddy Sinclaire's uncle and legal guardian over a substantial trust fund left by his parents. And according to Atkins, when Joker asked his uncle for the money, he refused to give it to him."

Skylar asked him, "Maxwell, don't tell me you're serious about all of this."

His reply was, "Skylar, I'm as serious as a throbbing toothache."

"Did Atkins happen to say why Chatsworth refused to give Joker the money?"

"Yes, he did. It appears that the parents and Chatsworth had a verbal agreement."

"Did Atkins also tell you what kind of agreement and why?" Skylar asked. Before Maxwell could reply to his questions, Skylar asked him to hold on for a second. He returned to the phone saying, "I'm sorry about the interruption. We're a little short-handed this evening. Now where were we?" he asked.

Maxwell said, "No apology is necessary. I understand. It appears that Chatsworth was to teach Joker the business and a sense of responsibility of how to use the money they'd left to establish a business of his own.

Apparently, they felt Chatsworth could straighten him out."

Skylar asked, "And you're saying Chatsworth is still holding onto the money?"

Maxwell said, "Precisely. In addition, I would venture to say when he ordered them off his property, Joker decided he wasn't leaving without first getting his money. Skylar, do you recall my telling you that I observed a sneaky grin on Joker's face when Chatsworth told them to get out of his sight?"

Skylar replied, "Yes, I remember so. In other words, Joker went back to collect and Chatsworth refused to give him the money."

Maxwell replied, "Yes, and remember the housekeeper's statement that she heard the other man tell Chatsworth that he wanted everything the he owed him?"

"Yes, I do recall her words and you're correct," Skylar replied.

Maxwell asked him, "Can you think of a stronger motivation for the shooting?"

Skylar replied, "No, and I'm inclined to agree with you, but there's still one thing I'm curious about."

"What is that?" Maxwell asked him.

Skylar said, "The car was found abandoned in Arleta. Where were they headed and why, Maxwell?"

He laughed and said, "I believe those are two questions, Skylar, but here's my scenario—I don't believe they were headed for any particular place unless there's someone else that no one knows about, and if they were, it would have only been for a short period. Perhaps that was as far away as he wanted to go which would have given him the time he needed to decide what his next move is going to be. Remember Joker is out of control and cunning, not stupid, which makes him even more dangerous. He's managed to elude the authorities by moving about under a cloak of darkness and what better way to throw them off track than to leave a false trail?"

For a full minute, Skylar was silent, then asked Maxwell, "Are you saying he's planning to do something else?"

Maxwell laughed and said, "Skylar, I'll bet you a Sunday's dinner he is, but I have no concept of what it might be. I believe the best we can hope for is he'll make his move soon and no one else gets hurt in the process."

"Well, I hope you're right because the Arleta police have not been able to come up with anything either. It's as if a ghost drove into town, parked the stolen car and left," Skylar said.

Maxwell said, "Yes, but we know it wasn't a ghost. I've some paperwork to go over and tomorrow I plan to do some scouting around,

I'll be in touch."

"I'll be looking forward to it," Skylar responded.

Looking at his wristwatch and noting the time, Maxwell thought to himself, gracious, there's no wonder I'm beginning to feel nauseous, it's been a while since I ate anything.

In addition, on that note, he stopped at a nearby restaurant and ordered a full-course dinner and a large Pepsi to take out. While driving the short distance to his office, he thought, this case with Chatsworth and Joker is really getting under my skin. If only there was some way to figure out what their next move is going to be. Chatsworth is still hospitalized so he can't be planning to approach him again or go anywhere near him, especially since they're being wanted by the authorities.

"Oh, well, for now I'm just going to enjoy my dinner while completing the paperwork, close shop, go home, take a warm relaxing shower and get a good night's sleep before another disruption occurs."

In the meanwhile, Steven Chatsworth had made a telephone call to Victor Atkins asking him if would be so kind as to come to the hospital. There were some personal matters that he wanted to discuss with him. He informed his nurse that he was expecting an important visitor and did not wish to be disturbed other than his physician, under any circumstances. Atkins arrived at the hospital within a half-hour's time, after receiving Chatsworth's call. He entered the room and was surprised to see Chatsworth sitting in a chair by the window.

Looking at him for a brief second, he asked him, "How are you feeling, Steven?"

He gazed at Atkins smiled and said, "I feel as if I've been run over by a bulldozer."

Atkins laughed and said, "Oh, well, you've always been a tough old buzzard anyway and it's good to see you up again, my friend."

He smiled and said, "Thanks, it certainly feels good to be up, but for a while there I must confess the odds seemed to have been against me."

After a brief period of silence, Atkins observed a rather disturbed expression appear on Chatsworth's face. Then, suddenly, looking into his eyes, he said, "Victor, I asked you to come because lying here in this bed has given me an opportunity to face up to certain things."

Atkins never interrupted; he just sat quietly and allowed him to speak.

Chatsworth said, "This shooting incident has allowed me the chance to put things in their perspective order. First and foremost, I should have taken the advice you were trying to give me when Freddy managed to get himself into trouble two years ago. Perhaps my ending up in the hospital as the result of his having shot me would have been averted. I realize that now and bear the responsibility of ignorance as well. You see, Victor, you never asked, but I'm quite certain you knew that young man whom he assaulted was paid handsomely by me not to make his appearance in the courts. That, my friend, was a huge error on my part. I should have insisted that Freddy assume responsibility for what he had done. I only thought, perhaps hoped, he would realize the seriousness of his offense and straighten himself out. I can clearly see now that was only a misconception on my part and now this. I refused to release the inheritance when he turned twenty-five solely because of the agreement between his parents and I. Even now, I don't believe he's really learned what it is to accept responsibility. He's gotten himself into a predicament that even I will not be able to get him out of."

Atkins stared at him and said, "Perhaps this is just what he needed, Steven, only much earlier."

He said, "You might be correct on that point, Victor." Then he paused for a moment and said, "Incidentally, I've been following the news and I'm very much aware of what he's been doing. First, he kills that young man, Stevenson, and carjacks someone else." With deep sadness in his eyes, he said to Victor, "I'm afraid Freddy's behavioral pattern began long before I agreed to become his legal guardian. My sister and her husband had spoiled him to the end and frankly, I believe they had lost control of him long ago. One day her husband telephoned me asking if we could have a talk. I said yes, and asked him when did he want to meet? This was perhaps two months prior to their deaths he said as soon as it was convenient for me. That is when we scheduled the meeting and the time. He came to the office, and we began to talk. As you know, Freddy's an only child because when he was born the doctors told them she could not survive another pregnancy. Oh, we managed to keep in touch while he was growing up, but never saw each other often. His job took him out of the country quite a bit, she often accompanied him, and Freddy went into boarding school, I believe when he was age twelve. According to his father, by the time he reached age fifteen, he literally had gone through three boarding schools. The reports received from each of them stated that he taunted and intimidated other students by pulling malicious pranks on them. After the last one, he and my sister both agreed that she should remain home for a while, but that didn't seem to resolve the problem. From that time on through high school, they found themselves getting him out of one incident after another. I didn't know at the time why he was desperately pleading with me to become Freddy's legal guardian. Victor, I really didn't know if I would be up to the challenge of an undisciplined and spoiled young man, so I asked them to give me time, to think about it. In the meanwhile, I thought they should explore any other options there might have been. Three days later, she telephoned me and said they discussed guardianship and realized I was their only hope that's when I contacted you. Now I regret things haven't worked out the way they so desperately wanted."

After looking into his eyes and seeing a great sadness, Atkins thought perhaps some of it might have been contributed to his feelings of guilt, which can sometimes become a heavy burden. He cleared his throat and said, "Steven you had nothing to do whatsoever with your nephew's upbringing. You only thought that in some way, you could help the three of them. When he came to you his convictions of right and wrong were already established. Frankly, I believe his parents were aware of this fact as well. Perhaps, they might have felt that your strong discipline would have influenced him to straighten himself up. Steven, now there's something else that I feel compelled to convey to you."

Chatsworth stared at him briefly and asked, "What is it, Victor?"

"Bradford T. Maxwell, a private investigator," Chatsworth snapped. "I know who he is, what about him?"

Atkins said, "We had a meeting."

Suddenly, Chatsworth said, "What?!" Then he asked Atkins, "A meeting about what Victor?"

At that point, Atkins saw his face become flushed and said, "Hold on, Steven, don't get your dandruff up. Maxwell somehow learned that I was the attorney who represented Freddy in the assault case and asked about it. You know as well as I do that when the victim suddenly disappeared just before the trial date, the aspect of it all was going to be questionable, to say the least. He was more interested in knowing how he could afford to pay a bail that was set at such an exuberant amount while working for you. And of course, who paid the attorney fees?"

"And what did you tell him?" Chatsworth asked.

"I told him the truth—you paid the bail and his attorney fees. Then he wanted to know why you would take on such a responsibility for an employee with no possible means of repaying that amount of money. I learned from him that he was concerned about you as well as I under the circumstances. That is when I told him about the inheritance and your relationship with Freddy."

In a rather staunch tone, Chatsworth said, "That was none of his business and why was he questioning you about it anyway?"

Atkins took a deep breath and exhaled. Focusing his eyes directly on Chatsworth, he said, "Listen to me for once in your stubborn life, Steven. Whether you like it or not, and you must face the fact that Freddy's out of control, Maxwell as well as the authorities are seeking a motive for his having shot you in the first place, and strongly believe that he's planning to do something else."

Chatsworth stared hard at him and asked, "Like what, for instance? I'm in the hospital and out of control or not, he's not foolish enough to come here."

Atkins replied, "No one knows, because he's very unpredictable. They've somehow managed to elude the authorities even with all of the roadblocks."

Chatsworth sighed and said, "Victor, one of Freddy's problems is and I believe has always been he was never encouraged to take responsibility for anything."

Atkins said, "Well, Steven, I'm afraid he will have to assume responsibility this time; he will have no choice."

Chatsworth said, "I'm sorry about the young man, Stevenson, though, and what puzzles me the most is, why did Freddy kill him anyway? The three of them came to my residence together, unless he'd promised them something. He really came there, assuming I'd release the inheritance to him. He said that he wanted everything that was his then! I wasn't about to give him the money to squander off that, wasn't what his parents had desired for him and I was only attempting to honor their request."

Atkins said, "Yes, Steven, and as a result, it nearly cost you your life."

Chatsworth had a look of despair on his face when he said, "I honestly don't believe he's going to surrender to the authorities voluntarily. I sincerely hope no one else will become another one of his victims in the process of their attempting to apprehend him, or he becomes one himself." After speaking, he turned his head and stared out the window for a few minutes, neither one spoke a word.

Suddenly, gazing into Atkins's eyes, he said, "Victor, I would very much appreciate it if you will do me a favor. I've been thinking about it quite extensively since being here. I believe it is time, for me to try and make amends for my negligence."

Atkins gazed at him, smiled and asked, "What is it, Steven? You know I will do whatever I can for you."

He said, "I would like very much for you to contact someone for me. He lives in Arleta, California. I'll give you his full name, address, and of course, the telephone number."

Atkins asked him, "How soon do you wish me to contact this person?"

Chatsworth smiled and said, "I would say, at your earliest convenience." He took a pad and pen off the bedside table and after writing the information down, he gave it to Atkins, who after reading it exclaimed, "Jumping Jupiter, Steven!"

The following morning Maxwell showered, shaved, and ate a hearty breakfast which he prepared himself that consisted of crisp bacon, over easy eggs, rye toast with jam, orange juice, and coffee. After ingesting his delectable breakfast, he drove to one of the construction sites he'd visited during his investigation, only this time, the reception was much different. It appeared that his arrival was well-timed.

He hadn't gotten out of his car when the man who warned him to leave the site and don't come back came rushing up to him, and said, "Maxwell, we just got a call from one of the other construction companies that one of their men has spotted that crazy Joker and Bishop jump off the back of a truck near the Santa Monica off-ramp."

Maxwell gazed at him and asked, "When was this?"

The man thought for a minute and said, "That was early this morning because we were just opening up the yard."

Maxwell then asked him, "Did the fellow say what kind of truck they jumped out of?"

"No, he just said that it looked like some kind of large white or grey company truck. He couldn't read the name on it and I sure hope they don't show up here."

Maxwell looked at him and said, "Thank you for the information at least; we know they're back in this area." He remained in his car watching the man as he slowly walked away. He picked up the car phone and dialed Skylar's cell number hoping to contact him at home since he's on the evening shift this week.

"Good morning, Maxwell. What can I do for you this early?"

"And a good morning to you, Skylar. I happen to have some good news to share with you for a change."

Skylar laughed and said, "Well, man, how long are you going to keep me in suspense?"

Maxwell said, "I was just informed that our two suspects were seen getting out of the back of a truck near the Santa Monica off-ramp early this morning. The man could only describe it as being some large white or grey company truck, he was unable to read the name on it." Skylar was silent for a minute, then said, "Maxwell, this means they're back in the area. Look, I'm going to alert the station with this information; maybe this is the break we've been looking for."

Maxwell said, "At least we know they're back in the area, but what we still don't know is what's going through his mind right now."

Skylar thought for a moment and said, "That's true, perhaps he'll make a move in our direction soon, but in the meanwhile, what are you planning to do? Some more scouting around?"

He gave a hearty laugh and asked, "How did you know, Skylar?"

"Because that's what you're good at doing, Maxwell, and in some ways, I envy you," Maxwell asked him why.

"Because you have the freedom to do it and in my position. I can't."

He said, "Well my friend, I suppose you have a point I can't argue with. I'll be in touch with you later."

"Joker, why are we still hanging around here? You want us to get caught by the cops, Bishop nervously said.

Joker gave him a hard stare and said, "Be quiet, stupid, I'm trying to figure out a way to get us a ride."

Bishop looked at him and asked, "What kind of ride? There's nothing out here but trucks and how are we going to make it out of here in a truck?"

Joker asked Bishop, "You see that dump truck parked over there by the building?" pointing to a building about ten feet away from where they were standing.

Bishop looked in the direction he was pointing and said, "Yeah, I see it, but how are you going to drive it out of here, Joker?"

He looked at Bishop and said, "Just follow me and be quiet, will you?"

Joker took off running in the direction of the truck and Bishop was following closely behind him. Opening the door on the driver's side while taking a swift look around them and getting into the truck, he looked over at Bishop, who was just standing there, and asked, "Are you getting in or not?"

Without saying a word, he immediately complied. By that time, Joker had already started the motor and as Bishop was closing the door, he was driving off. Bishop looked at him and said, "Joker, we're not getting out of here without being seen."

At that point, Joker said, "Just watch me and see." Other trucks were coming in and going out beginning their routes. As a truck loaded with cement and a mixer drove out of the gate, so did Joker.

When they'd gone a short distance away from the site, Bishop said, "I cannot believe we just stole a big dump truck from a construction company. Boy, they're really going to be looking for us now."

Joker started to laugh and said, "Yeah, but not before we get to where we're going." Bishop was afraid to ask, but he did anyway. "Just where are we going, Joker?"

"Where do you think stupid?" Bishop looked hard at him and his heart did a flip-flop because of the direction they were going he knew the answer, but asked anyway. "Not back to your uncle's place?"

Joker laughed and said, "He's still in the hospital and I know where the safe is; I'm going to get what is rightfully mine and that's that!"

Bishop thought to himself, he's really nuts. Lord, I wish there were some way I could get away from this lunatic before he gets the both of us killed. What if the cops are waiting for us out there? I'd rather take my chances with them than him.

As they were getting near Chatsworth's residence, Bishop was becoming more nervous, but he didn't say anything. Suddenly, Joker began to drive faster. He looked at him and said, "Oh, Lord, no!"

Following a hunch on something, he recalled Maxwell went to another construction site that he'd visited doing his investigation. As he arrived and was parking his car, he observed the gathering of a small group of workers and wondered to himself, what's going on here? Little did he realize that the answer to his question was forthcoming as he began to walk toward them. They all turned to face him in unison and the foreman approached him looking as if he'd seen a ghost. The man informed him that the duo had been there earlier apparently, on one of their supply trucks. The foreman stated that they looked as if they'd been in the swamp somewhere and smelled like a chicken yard, he went on to say, everyone knew what had happened and didn't want anything to do with either of them.

He said, "I must admit, I did feel kind of sorry for Bishop though."

Maxwell looked at him and asked, "Why is that?"

He said, "Because he looked as if you blew too hard, he'd fall down."

Maxwell gazed at him and asked, "What happened?"

The man said, "Joker was desperately trying to get one of the guys to loan him his car."

"And did he?" Maxwell asked.

"The fellow lied and told him that he was just getting ready to take his wife to the hospital. He was always coming out here playing silly jokes on the men until the boss finally was fed up with it and threatened to report him to Chatsworth. This is the first time that we've seen him in about a couple of weeks. Then we heard the police were looking for them in the Chatsworth shooting and the other guy that was always with them. Is it true that he killed him?"

Maxwell said, "Yes, that's true."

"My gracious man, no wonder Joker was acting like a raving maniac when they showed up here. Staring steadily at him, Maxwell asked the foreman, "How do you mean?"

"He kept yelling that Chatsworth owed him and he was going to get everything that belonged to him."

"Chatsworth is still in the hospital. Just how does he plan to get it?" Maxwell questioned.

"He said, that's the strange part about it. I don't know and he never said."

Maxwell said, "I see. And what was Bishop saying while all of Joker's raving was going on?" His reply was, "He never said anything; you could tell he's deathly afraid of Joker."

Maxwell asked, "Where did they go after leaving here?"

"Man, I honestly don't have any idea where they might have gone, as long as it's away from here. The men just started walking away and the next thing anybody knew they'd vanished." "No one saw them leave?" he asked.

"No, everybody was too anxiously trying to get away from them as quickly as they possibly could. The boss wanted to call the police, but by the time he'd made up his mind he was told by one of the guys they were gone, and I guess he was thinking good riddance."

Maxwell said, "I see," musing to himself that they didn't just walk out of here somehow, they had help.

Just as he was about to speak with the owner, a man came running towards them yelling, "Where's the boss?"

The foreman he was talking with pointed in the direction of the office. He and Maxwell stared at each other in total bewilderment as the man quickly snatched open the door and ran inside. A few minutes had lapsed when the man and the boss came out running in their direction. That time, it was the boss who was doing the yelling. "That crazy Joker and the imbecile with him has stolen one of my dump trucks."

Maxwell stared at the three of them, then in a rather stern tone asked, "And no one around here saw them leave, not to mention a heavy vehicle such as a dump truck?"

The foreman said, "We have equipment coming in and going out throughout the day; this is a construction site, remember?"

Maxwell replied, "Yes, I'm aware of that, but what is puzzling to me is how did they manage to take a vehicle that size out of here without anyone seeing them?"

The foreman spoke and said, "If anyone did see the truck, they probably assumed it was one of our drivers going on his run, and paid no attention."

Speaking to the driver who first came yelling, "When did you discover the truck was missing?"

The man said, "I was doing some paperwork in another building, and when I came out to make my scheduled trip, it was gone."

Maxwell looked at his wristwatch and estimated the time to have been a half-hour and forty-five minutes. He had been talking with the foreman for around a half-hour to give or take a few minutes before the theft was discovered. The foreman defensively said, "I explained that everyone was trying to get away from them; who would have ever thought they would be taking a big truck out of here?"

Maxwell looked at him and said, "Yes, I remember and I agree with you. Under the circumstances, I don't blame them. Perhaps it's a good thing no one did catch them in the act; he could have quite easily become another victim."

Turning his attention to the owner, he said, "I'm going to alert the Santa Monica Police Department. They will also need the identification information on your truck."

Without hesitation, the owner said, "Sure, come with me to my office."

Following the owner into his office, Maxwell asked permission to use the telephone on his desk. "Man, I don't know where they could be going, but I sure hope they don't wreck my truck," then he immediately walked across the room to a very large grey file cabinet. In the meanwhile, Maxwell was making contact with Detective Skylar, who informed him that he was having the call transferred to his supervisor's office. Once the connection was made, he apprised them of everything that had transpired up to and including his present whereabouts. He also gave them the information on the stolen truck. Then he addressed Skylar, specifically asking him, "Do you recall our conversation when I told you there was something not right about this situation?"

He replied, "Yes, I remember quite well."

Then Maxwell repeated what the foreman had told him regarding Joker's demeanor and words. "Skylar, number one, Chatsworth's still in the hospital, so how in the world can he expect to collect anything from him?"

Skylar's response was, "Yes, that's correct."

Then Maxwell asked him, "Number two, what would you need with a big dump truck if you're just trying to escape from the authorities?"

There was a brief pause then the supervisor's voice came in. He asked, "Wait a minute, Maxwell, are you telling us that those maniacs are planning to use that truck to break into Chatsworth's residence?" He replied, "Yes, I believe so. Can you conceive of a more appropriate solution?"

Then he said, "Now we know what he's been planning to do all along and how he's going to accomplish it."

After hearing that statement, the supervisor exclaimed, "Oh my word!"

Maxwell asked in a concerned tone, "Where's the housekeeper right now?"

Skylar said, "She's living in Hermosa Beach with relatives until

Chatsworth's recovered enough to be discharged home." "That's the good news," Maxwell said.

The supervisor said, "Listen, Maxwell, we're on top of this situation as we speak. I pray we can get to them before too much damage is done to the man's residence."

Maxwell said, "So do I, but I don't know. From my estimation, they've got a fairly good head start."

After a brief pause, Skylar said, "Maxwell."

"Don't you fret, Skylar? I'm quite familiar with departmental procedures. I'll remain away and let you men perform your job."

"Thanks! I'll be in touch with you when all of this has been resolved, no matter what."

"Fine by me," he said smiling to himself.

While waiting for the authorities to complete their job, his inner thoughts were of the two suspects. *I don't believe they'll have much trouble out of Bishop, that is, if they can somehow manage to separate him from Joker; he's the dominant influence. In addition, as far as he's concerned, that's an entirely different story because from all indications, he's like a person with 'tunnel vision'. He's focused straight ahead on whatever it is he's trying to accomplish. It doesn't matter to him who's involved or gets hurt and he's not going to give up without a fight. Joker has really gone off the deep end and it's too bad if they can't resolve the situation without it resulting in his death. I'm certain they will do everything that is reasonably possible to prevent that happening. He needs to learn that life is precious and not a 'joke' after all. I'd better telephone Blake and bring him up to date on the situation, especially, since he's responsible for my having become involved in it to begin with.*

"Thank you very much. That is very pleasant news, indeed." Blake had just completed his call to the hospital and was informed that Steven Chatsworth's condition had greatly improved. In fact, he was allowed to have visitors for a short period. Then his thoughts reverted to Maxwell and with an amused grin on his face, he wondered how he and Detective Skylar had gotten along. The telephone rang and Jenny informed him that Mr. Maxwell was on the line. He asked her to put him through and she immediately complied. "Hello, Brad, I was wondering how you and Detective Skylar have been getting along," he said with a mischievous grin on his face.

"Yes, I'll bet you were," he said laughing.

"Well, I've got some good news for you," Blake told him.

"Oh, what is it this time? Are you planning to sic someone else on me?" Laughing loudly, he asked, "Now why would I do something like that?" "Blake Colwell, that's your nature, buddy."

"Oh, I see," he said. "Are you interested in hearing the good news for a change or not?"

"I certainly am," was his reply to Blake's question.

"I was on the telephone with the hospital a short while ago, and was informed that Chatsworth's condition has greatly improved. In fact, his physician is allowing him to have visitors for short periods of time."

"Now that is what I consider good news. I knew the old buzzard was too mean and ornery to just give up that way."

"I'm inclined to agree with you, Brad. Perhaps we can finally get this pickled situation that has stalemated us for so long resolved."

"Now that my friend is an enlightening concept, nothing would please me more," he said.

"Well, fellow, how long are you going to keep me in suspense? What has happened since we last spoke?" Maxwell apprised him of all the recent events that had occurred. Now he was just waiting for the authorities to resolve the situation.

Blake laughed so hard that he gasped, then asked, "Do you mean to tell me that they allowed a big dump truck to be driven from beneath their very noses?"

"Yes, that is precisely what happened. It appears that everyone was so preoccupied with trying to escape from the pair that stealing a big truck never occurred to anyone."

"Tell me, Brad, what influenced your belief that the two were going to Chatsworth's residence?"

"Blake, when I began to backtrack the situation, number one, the housekeeper stated that she overheard an argument in which one of the men told Chatsworth that he wanted everything that belonged to him. Somehow, I never paid into the speculation that Joker was a disgruntled ex-employee who was just out to settle the score for having been terminated. Although these things happen more frequently than we care to admit to me, it just didn't apply in this case. Number two, when I questioned the foreman at the construction company, he stated that Joker was raving and ranting about Chatsworth owing him a lot of money and he planned to collect it. Then I recalled the meeting with Atkins and the information that he conveyed to me regarding the money and what had actually transpired between Chatsworth and Joker. The motive had to be money. Since Chatsworth is still hospitalized, how could he collect anything from him? There has to be something in his home that Joker feels he can get his hands on and at this point, no one really knows, only Joker himself and perhaps Bishop. The foreman also stated that Joker had tried desperately to get one of the men to loan him his car, but the man lied, saying he was getting ready to take his wife to the hospital. When it was discovered, the truck had been stolen, that's when it hit me like a neon light. I knew they had some sort of help getting out of there unobserved, but taking a dump truck never occurred to me either. Not only were they using the truck as a means of transportation, but also to break into the man's residence."

"Brad, are you saying they're going to use it as a sort of ramming vehicle?"

"I believe so. He's gone wild and it doesn't matter to him how much damage is done."

"Good gracious!" Blake exclaimed. "He really has lost it, hasn't he?"

"I'm afraid so, Blake, but the ironic thing about this whole episode is, unlike Joker, the fellow who is involved in it with him doesn't even have a police record that is up until now."

"What! Then how did he manage to get himself involved with a maniac like Joker?"

"That is my sentiment exactly, Blake. After going through all of this, I would imagine he would be asking himself that same question. Perhaps, we'll get some answers from him when this is over."

"So, what are you planning to do now?" Blake asked him.

He replied, "For the moment, nothing until I hear from Skylar and his people. I'm waiting for an opportunity to have a talk with Chatsworth and find out what position he prefers to take in the firm's situation."

"Yes, I understand what you mean, Brad, and I'm in complete agreement with you on this."

"Listen, Blake, I'll get back to you later."

"That will be fine, Brad, and thanks for the update."

"As usual, you're welcome, Blake."

Maxwell returned to his office to complete some unfinished paperwork. After spending a couple of hours there and feeling tension in his muscles, he decided to close shop and go down to the gym for a good workout. In the meanwhile, the authorities were en route to Steven Chatsworth's residence. They knew the two suspects had undoubtedly arrived there ahead of them according to Maxwell's information. Arriving cautiously because they had no idea what was transpiring there or, for that matter, what to expect. However, there was a known fact that the duo was desperate and desperate people seldom think rationally. At that point, all they could do was remain alert. As they were slowly approaching the residence, someone in the group exclaimed, "Man! Look at that place and where's the truck?"

Early the next morning as he was getting into his car, the phone began to ring, and looking at the display he said, "Good morning, Skylar, and just what can I do for you this morning?"

"Good morning to you, Maxwell, have you had breakfast?"

"No, not yet, why?"

Skylar said, "There's a quaint little restaurant called the Galaxy near the station. And their breakfast menu is superb." "Yes, I know the one you're speaking of," Maxwell said.

"Then how about joining me there?" Skylar asked him.

"What time?" he asked him.

"How about now? I'm officially off duty until tomorrow morning."

"It's a deal and I'll see you in about twenty minutes."

"Mr. Colwell, Mrs. Carrington is on the line, sir."

"Please put her through, Jenny."

"Yes, sir."

"Claudia, my dear, what a pleasant surprise. When did you return from your trip?" he asked her.

She replied, "It's good to hear your voice too, Blake. I arrived home late last night."

Blake asked her, "How was your stay in Italy?"

She replied, "Oh, Blake, it was just fabulous, and I had a marvelous time."

He said, "That's wonderful and you sound great, Claudia."

"I feel great too. Blake, what in the world has been going on in my absence?"

"What do you mean, my dear?"

"Don't you dare 'my dear' me, that is your way of avoiding my question as usual you sly old fox. You know precisely what I mean!" she said laughing. "Early this morning I saw a special news report on television, and it was reported that two of the three men involved in the Chatsworth shooting were apprehended at his home last evening. Blake, they showed a big dump truck that had plowed through the man's home. It looked as if a tornado had been through there. There was a confrontation with the police by one of the suspects (Blake instantly thought to himself, that would have been Joker) who sustained minor injuries, and both are now in police custody for questioning. Blake, how is Chatsworth and when did all of this take place?"

"Claudia, to answer your first question, according to the hospital medical staff, his condition is improving, and to answer question number two, all of this transpired within the past seventy-two hours. It's a long story, I can assure you so. After you've gotten some rest, how about coming to the office? This way it will be easier for me to give you all of the details," he told her.

She said, "Oh, all right. Will you be available later this afternoon around two-thirty?"

"Yes, that will be good timing. I'll see you then," he told her.

After consuming a hearty breakfast, Skylar and Maxwell sat back sipping on their coffee. Skylar said, "Man, your assessment of those two suspects was correct; you were right on the mark."

"What happened out there, Skylar?" Maxwell asked.

Skylar looked at him and said, "What first hit all of us in the face when we were approaching the residence was this huge gapping opening in the front of the house. Then one of the guys asked, 'Where's the truck?' Because none of us saw it, that is, until we got closer. There was this big dump truck that had literally gone through the front section of the building and stopped near the rear section of the house. Glass and lumber were still falling because the house had been compromised by the impact. Maxwell, it appeared as if a tornado had just passed through there and the roof was still collapsing. A perimeter was set up around the entire estate. After everyone was in their assigned position of course you're familiar with the procedure following that."

Maxwell said, "Yes, I am."

"Mind you, there was still no sign of the two and no indication of just where they might have been. Man, do you know we were out there nearly four hours before there was any kind of response from them? The supervisor in charge decided we were just going to wait it out and let them make the first move. Finally, we spotted this figure crawling on top of all this rubble, like a large cat along the side of the house."

Maxwell began to laugh and so did Skylar, saying, "About ten feet from the house, he stood up, raising both hands above his head. With the spotlight shining on him, we knew it was Flint Bishop. He was ordered to turn around and walk backward to us. As soon as he was within arms' reach, he was told to lie face down with his arm stretched out. While three of the guys had their weapons trained on him, he was cuffed. There was no resistance from him at all. In fact, he seemed relieved to have been out there. He said that he had to get away somehow because Joker had flipped out, all he kept talking about was getting what was owed to him. He told the supervisor that when he last saw him, he was trying to break into Chatsworth's safe and that's when he saw a chance to escape. My guess is he looked around, didn't see Bishop, and probably tried to locate him and when he couldn't, he realized that he'd left him because suddenly, we heard this yelling coming from inside. I still can't imagine what prompted him to come through the broken window yelling and banishing the gun in all directions. That's when he was ordered to drop it, but instead, he started firing. He was wounded in the shoulder and leg by one of the sharpshooters. He'll recover to stand trial on these cases."

"A-men," Maxwell agreed. After a brief silence, Maxwell observed a puzzled expression appear on Skylar's face and asked him, "Skylar, is something wrong?"

He gazed at him and said, "Maxwell, there is one thing I can't figure out about those two."

"And just what is that, Skylar?"

"The both of them smelled as if they had been hibernating with poultry. I mean, the mere smell of them was nauseating." Maxwell looked at him for a minute recalling what the foreman at the construction company had said. Then he said, "Skylar, it's strange that you should say that. Because when I was questioning the foreman at the construction company where they stole the truck from, he said they looked as if they'd been in a swamp somewhere and smelled like a poultry yard." Skylar said, "That's the same description I would've given them. "Maxwell, I wonder where they were after their disappearance from this area. And if I recall our conversation correctly, didn't you state that someone had seen them earlier jump off some kind of company truck?"

"Yes, that's correct, Skylar, and why was the stolen car found abandoned in Arleta?"

He said, "You know, Maxwell, you've got a point there."

Maxwell thought for a moment and said, "Skylar, this situation is becoming more complicated by the minute. There are still loopholes that need to be filled in order to bring resolve."

Skylar asked him," You're referring to the time-lapse, am I correct?"

"Yes, I am," Maxwell replied."

Skylar gazed at him and said, "I hadn't thought of it in those terms, but since you mentioned it, perhaps we have the answers to those questions right before our eyes."

Maxwell said, "Man, I'm ready, let's hear it."

Skylar said, "Get this, will you?"

Bishop was more than ready to talk! The interrogating officer in charge was Detective Stefon Hauser. First, he asked, "Bishop, why did the three of you go back to Mr. Chatsworth's residence?" That's when Bishop opened the valve and said, "He wasn't about to become anybody's scapegoat and was ready to talk. I waited around the room for a few minutes as they were setting up for his statement, then I thought I'd better get out and let him do his job."

In answer to Detective Hauser's question, Bishop said, "Joker told Stevenson and him that since Mr. Chatsworth had told them to get off his property and stay off, he owed him a lot of money and he wanted all of it! Then he was asked, 'Why did the two of you go back there with him after you were told to stay away?' He said, 'Because Joker told us that he was going to split with us when he got the money'." "And you believed him?" he was asked.

He replied, "Yes, both of us did."

"Tell us exactly what happened when you arrived there."

"Well, when we first got there, Joker rang the doorbell and Mr. Chatsworth came to the door and when he saw us, he looked at Joker and asked him, "What do you want?" Then he turned his back and started walking away; Joker followed him into the study. Stevenson and me, we stayed outside in the hallway."

"Go on, what happened when they went into the study?"

"We heard Mr. Chatsworth yell and say, 'I told you once to get out and stay out, and I meant it!' Then he asked Joker, 'Now what are you doing back here?' Joker told him, 'I want everything that's mine now!' Mr.

Chatsworth yelled again, 'Get out of here!' Joker looked at him and started laughing like crazy, then all of a sudden, we saw him pull out his gun and that's when Stevenson and me took off and started running back to the car. That's when we heard the shots and I told him, 'Man, he's gone crazy; we never should've come back here with him'."

Bishop was then asked, "About how many shots did you hear?"

He said, "Man, I don't know, maybe three or four, I'm not sure; we just wanted to get out of there. The next thing we knew, Joker came running out the door with the gun still in his hand and told us to get in the car quickly. Neither one of us asked him any questions because we knew what had happened, but we didn't know he was going to shoot the old man."

He was asked, "What did the three of you do after you left the Chatsworth's residence?"

"Joker drove around for a while; he just kept saying, 'He should've given me what's mine.' By that time, we were really worried and scared because we didn't know what he was going to do next, he was acting like a wild man. We finally ended up at a bar by the pier where we go sometimes."

Det. Hauser asked him, "How long were you in the bar?"

Bishop said, "Maybe about an hour. We drank a couple of beers, then Joker said, 'Let's go'. We started walking down towards the pier and I guess Stevenson had had enough because he asked Joker, 'Why did you have to shoot the old man?' Joker just looked at him and said, 'He brought it on himself; he should've given me my money'. I could tell Stevenson was really getting scared because he said, 'Now you're going to have the cops looking for all of us because you went crazy out there, and still didn't get any money. You two can do whatever you want, but I'm leaving. Joker wouldn't hear of it and told him that, 'Nobody is getting out'. That's when he pulled out the gun and shot Stevenson. When he turned and tried to run away, he shot him again in the back. By that time, I was too scared to say anything because he was laughing like crazy."

Det. Hauser looked at him and asked, "What did you do after Stevenson was shot?"

Bishop said, "I didn't do anything. I was so scared I guess I just froze because the next thing I knew, Joker was yanking me by the arm saying, 'Let's get out of here', and we started running. I didn't know where we were going and didn't care just as long as it was away from there and poor Stevenson."

Det. Hauser gazed at Bishop for a couple of seconds, then asked him, "Tell me, Bishop, whose idea was it to carjack that man at the service station, and why an old man?" He looked down at the floor for a brief minute, then slowly focused his eyes directly on Det. Hauser, and said, "It was Joker's idea. He said that way we could go back to his car because the cops would be looking for it, so we needed a ride to get out of there." With a remorseful expression on his face, Bishop said, "I thought maybe he was looking for a car someplace to just 'hot-wire' and drive off. It never occurred to me that he was planning all along to carjack somebody. So, when we got to a service station he looked around and there was no one outside but this old man who was just getting into his car. Before I could think about it, he started running up to the car, snatching the old man out and throwing him to the ground, while holding the gun to his head. I thought for sure he was going to shoot him. I believe if he had tried to fight back, Joker would've shot him too. I felt sorry for him and started to get sick to my stomach."

"And what happened after that?" Det. Hauser asked him.

Bishop said, "He jumped into the car yelling, 'Hurry up and get in the car stupid'.

"What did you do then?" he was asked.

Bishop said, "I did what he said and got in the car; he was still holding the gun."

"Bishop, I'm rather curious about something: where did you and Joker go after you left the service station?"

He replied, "Joker said we had to get out of the area and fast, so we jumped on the 101 freeway. I asked him where we were going because the cops were going to be looking for the car. He laughed and said that he knew of a place where they wouldn't be looking for us."

Det. Hauser asked him, "Where was this place, Bishop?"

Bishop stared hard at him for a few seconds and said, "Look, Detective, Joker has hurt people. I don't want to be responsible for hurting anyone, especially since they had nothing to do with what he's done."

There was a brief period of silence in the room. Det. Hauser gazed hard into his eyes and said, "Bishop, whether you believe this or not is entirely up to you, but we're not out to deliberately hurt anyone; we're just trying to get to the bottom of this situation."

With that having been said, it was quite obvious that he was becoming nervous and after a period of silence he said, "We went to Joker's cousin's home in Arleta."

Det. Hauser stared at him and asked, "Did you say Joker's cousin's home?"

Bishop looked at him and said, "Yeah, why'd you ask?"

Det. Hauser fingered through his notes, then looked at Bishop again, saying, "There's nothing here in Joker's files stating he has relatives anywhere. Are you speaking the truth about this, he asked him?"

Bishop stared directly into his eyes and said, "I'm telling you the truth. I didn't think he had any kin either because he never spoke about it, but when finally arrived there, I learned that not only does he have a cousin, he also an uncle—the one he shot, Mr. Chatsworth."

With that revelation, Det. Hauser pushed his chair back, stood up, and exclaimed, "What?!"

Bishop said, "Yeah, that's right, Mr. Steven Chatsworth is Joker's uncle. I learned this during their conversation while we were there."

After that, Det. Hauser returned to his chair and slowly sitting down he said, "My gracious, this situation is becoming more outrageous by the minute," as he was slowly absorbing in disbelief what had just been revealed to him. Finally, he looked across the table at Bishop and asked him, "What is the name of Joker's cousin?"

Bishop was somewhat hesitant at first, then he said, "Joker only introduced him to me as John D. and that's all I ever heard."

"What happened while you two were there?" Det. Hauser asked him. Bishop, who had been leaning slightly over the table since the onset of the interrogation, suddenly sat straight up in the chair. And for the first time, there was a composed expression on his face when he said, "We were only there until it was dark, but just long enough for me to learn about Joker and Mr. Chatsworth. I could tell that Joker was becoming anxious to leave anyway."

"Why do you say that, Bishop?"

"Because he didn't like what John D. was saying and he's the only man that I ever saw stand up to Joker. When I first saw him, I wondered to myself, was he as loony as Joker, but other than their physical appearances, there is no similarity between the two."

Det. Hauser asked, "I'm not following you, Bishop. Just what are you saying?"

He said, "They look enough alike to be mistaken for identical twins, but John D. is more serious, mature, and open-spoken. He doesn't care for the predicament that Joker has gotten himself into and he straight out told him so. Then he really started talking and that's when everything came out."

Det. Hauser asked him, "What do you mean by everything?"

Bishop said, "Well, the first thing was when Joker told John D. that there is only one other person out there that knows about him and he's in the hospital. I started to wonder to myself because the only person in the hospital that I know of is Mr. Chatsworth, but how could he possibly know about John D.? In addition, the big shocker came when John D. asked Joker, 'Just what did happen between him and the old man?' Joker told him that Mr. Chatsworth had him do all of his dirty work and when it got too hot, he fired him."

Det. Hauser said, "Wait a minute. You said Joker told his cousin that Chatsworth had him do all of his dirty work. Just what did he mean by that, Bishop?"

He looked at him and said, "Well, Mr. Chatsworth had ordered us to do something that just wasn't right. And because of it he was being investigated, that's when he got angry and told us to get off his property."

Det. Hauser asked him, "Whom was he being investigated by and why?"

Bishop said, "I don't know for sure, but the day it happened, some private investigator had come to his home and talked to him."

Det. Hauser was writing something down on his notepad as Bishop was talking. When he had finished writing, he told Bishop to continue.

Bishop said, "John D. told Joker that Mr. Chatsworth couldn't fire him because he wasn't someone who was just working for him. Then he gave Joker a hard look and asked him, 'Is that what the shooting was about?'" "What was the shooting about, Bishop?"

"Joker said the shooting wasn't about his trying to fire him because he knew he couldn't. He told him to leave and don't come back. Then he said he didn't care about that, but he wanted everything that was his and when he told Mr. Chatsworth that, he refused. He told John D. that he went back for his to release his inheritance, not to shoot him, but when Mr. Chatsworth flatly told him to get out, Joker said that's when he just lost it and shot him."

Det. Hauser asked, "Wait a minute, are you saying that Joker shot Chatsworth over his inheritance?"

Bishop said, "Yes, but we—that is, Stevenson and I—didn't know anything about an inheritance at the time of the shooting."

Det. Hauser said, "So the motive for Chatsworth having been shot had to do with the inheritance." After a brief period of silence, he told Bishop to continue.

Bishop began by saying, "John D. told Joker he was sorry it had come to that, that there should have been some way for him to reason with him. After all, he is his uncle. Man, at that point I was becoming loose at the end because I finally realized why Joker was always trying to put Stevenson down, but he's the one who's nuts. John D. told Joker, 'You're lucky the old man's not dead, and let's face it, he is your legal guardian like it or not because that's the way your folks had it set up. What he couldn't understand is why Mr. Chatsworth didn't release the money last year when he turned twenty-five. Joker asked John D. why his parents chose his uncle anyway because as long as he could remember, he'd been a stickler for perfection. John D. told him that he probably wasn't going to like what he was about to say, but he would tell him anyway and he did. He told Joker that he didn't think anyone else wanted the responsibility of having to deal with him, even his parents said that he was irresponsible and to him, everything in life was a joke. He said that Joker was spoiled rotten and as a result, they were always bailing him out of one incident or another because he was constantly pulling those stupid pranks on people and laughing it off as a joke. That's when I thought to myself, so that's why he's called Joker.

"After what John D. had said even then, he said, 'But no one was ever seriously hurt'. John D. just looked at him and shook his head. But the next time he spoke, his tone was different. In fact, I'd admit it was rather stern at that time and seemed to have also caught Joker's attention because he just stared hard at him.

"He told Joker that it was time for him to grow up and assume responsibility for his own actions. Then he asked Joker, 'Has it ever occurred to you that the old man, Mr. Chatsworth, feels that he isn't ready for the responsibility of handling the inheritance yet?' Then Joker asked him, 'What is he supposed to do?' That's when John D. Told him that he was in a lot of trouble and the only one who can straighten it out is himself, and for once in his life, he should think about it. But you know, all the while John D. was talking, I was looking at Joker; he wasn't listening to what his cousin was saying, only the fastest way of getting out of there was the only thing on his mind."

A few minutes later, Det. Hauser asked Bishop, "What did you and Joker do after his cousin had finished talking to him?"

At that point, Bishop really didn't think John D. deserved to be involved in their predicament so he deliberately avoided giving out all of the details to the Det. He looked at Det. Hauser and said, "By that time, it was dark. We had to get out of there fast anyway before his wife came home. I gathered she didn't care for Joker because he'd already told Joker that if she came home and saw us, there would be the devil to pay. Joker just told John D. that we were leaving before she came home."

"Where did you two go after leaving John D.'s house?" Det. Hauser asked him.

"Joker drove around until he spotted this car wash that was closed, and he said that was a good place to leave the car because it wouldn't be opened up until the next morning. Besides, there was a rest area not far from there. We made our way to it and just as we got there a poultry truck was getting ready to pull out, Joker stopped him and paid the man fifty dollars to let us ride in the back of his truck. At first, he looked at us kind of funny. Joker showed him the money, he looked at it, then at us, just shrugged his shoulders, went to the back of the truck, unlocked the door, and told us to get in."

Suddenly, Det. Hauser burst out laughing and asked, "So that's why the two of you smell like a poultry farm."

At that remark, Bishop lowered his head and sheepishly responded, "Yes."

He asked Bishop, "Where did you go after that?"

He said, "We got out of the truck near the Santa Monica freeway off-ramp and hitched a ride to one of the construction companies where we use to hang out, the one that Joker stole the dump truck from." "Why a big dump truck, Bishop?" he asked him.

Bishop said, "At first, Joker tried to get one of the guys to let him use his car, but he couldn't get it. By that time, he was becoming furious and he spotted the truck in the back of a building. The driver was nowhere in sight, so he just grabbed it." Then Bishop said, "I believe Joker just wanted to destroy Mr. Chatsworth's home anyway."

Det. Hauser was silent for a while, then said, "I've been thinking, you know that aiding and abetting fugitives from justice is considered a criminal offense. However, according to what you have stated, John D. appears to be an honorable man who believes in fair play. What you've conveyed here has provided us with some valuable information. Since the two of you didn't remain there, and he didn't assist you in avoiding the authorities in any way, I can't see any reason why it would be necessary to bring him into this. Besides, we have all we need and I believe in this case, we can just say he was unfortunate enough to be caught up in something that he was not a part of."

He made a deep sigh, looked at Bishop, and said, "We're nearly done here, but I'm very curious about something, Bishop. There's no record of you having ever been involved with the law, that is, until now. How and why did you and Stevenson become involved with Sinclaire in the first place?"

Bishop looked directly into the detective's eyes when he said, "I've wished many times over that, I had never set eyes on him. Stevenson and I were looking for employment and we met him at one of the local bars where we used to hang out. After a few times there, one day Joker came up and told Stevenson and me that he could get us a job paying good money working for Mr. Chatsworth. We had no idea that he was nuts until we began to see some of the idiotic jokes he was playing on people. The strangest thing about it though was he seemed to thrive on it. Oh, we thought about leaving a couple of times, but Mr. Chatsworth paid us good money, so we stayed. With a remorseful expression on his face, he said if we had left, maybe Stevenson would be alive now."

Det. Hauser stared at him for a long while and thought to himself. *How is it that people like this young man sometimes, end up in a situation of this sort, who has never been in trouble with the law before and now has a record?* Finally, he said, "Well, that's all Bishop and thank you, you've been very helpful to us." Bishop looked at him and said,

"You're welcome, Detective Hauser."

They had finished breakfast and were slowly sipping on their coffee when Maxwell asked Skylar, "Was anyone successful in getting anything out of Joker?"

"Are you kidding? All he keeps babbling about is, 'He owes me a lot of money and I'm going to get it'.

Maxwell said, "Well, it appears that the joke is on him after all!'

"And rightfully so," Skylar said."

As Maxwell allowed his back to rest against the booth, he looked at Skylar smiled, and asked, "Now that's over what are you going to do next, Detective?"

But before Skylar had a chance to respond to Maxwell's question, his cell phone rang, and looking at Maxwell questioningly, he said, "This is Detective Jacob Skylar."

The caller said, "Detective Skylar, this is Stefon Hauser, I understand you're off duty, but will it be an imposition for me to have a talk with you as soon as possible?" Looking across the table at Maxwell in bewilderment and shrugging his shoulders he responded, no Det. Hauser it's not an imposition. Where are you now?" Skylar inquired.

He responded, "I'm still at the station, I've just completed the interrogation with Flint Bishop which is why I'm anxious to talk to you."

Skylar said, "I understand and I'm down the street from the station at the Galaxy restaurant; we can meet here if you like."

"That's fine with me. I'll be there in about ten minutes and thanks.

"You're welcome, was his response." Skylar gave Maxwell a grin and said, "let's see how the interrogation went, shall we?" Maxwell laughed and said, "this should prove to be quite interesting, to say the least."

Soon after entering the restaurant, Det. Hauser spotted Maxwell and Skylar sitting in a booth and made his way towards them. Skylar moved over to allow space for Hauser to sit. After the introduction, they ordered a fresh round of coffee. Hauser declined breakfast, stating he'd eaten earlier.

Skylar said, "I've explained to Maxwell that you're the interrogation officer in this case, which he's been active in since the onset."

Det. Hauser said, "This has been the most frustrating case that I've seen in a long time, it had more twists and turns than a maze."

Skylar looked at Maxwell and they both began to laugh, then Maxwell said, "Welcome to the club, Det."

Skylar looked at Hauser and asked him, "How did the interrogation go with Bishop?"

Det. Hauser said, "Well, gentlemen, it went a lot better than I had anticipated because Bishop filled in a few empty spaces. To begin with, according to Bishop's statements, he said he and Stevenson followed Sinclaire (Joker) back to the Chatsworth's residence because he told them that, since Chatsworth had ordered them off his property he owed him a lot of money and he wanted it all. In addition, he was going to split with them when he got it, and they believed him.

"When they arrived at the residence, Chatsworth met them at the door, looked at Joker, and asked him what he wanted. However, before Joker could answer him, he turned his back and started walking away. Joker followed him into the study.

"According to Bishop, he and Stevenson remained in the hallway. They heard Chatsworth yell saying, 'I told you once to get out and stay out, and I meant it!' Then he asked, 'Joker, now what are you doing back here?'

"Bishop said they heard Joker tell him that he wanted everything that was his. Then Chatsworth yelled again, 'Get out of here!' He said Joker looked at him and started laughing like crazy, then all of a sudden, they saw him pull out his gun. That's when he and Stevenson took off and started running back to the car.

"That's when they heard shots being fired and he told Stevenson's man, 'He's gone crazy'. He was asked, 'How many shots did you hear?' He said he didn't know, maybe three or four, he wasn't sure; they just wanted to get out of there. The next thing they knew he came running out the door with the gun in his hand and told them to get in the car quick. Bishop said neither of them asked any questions because they knew what had happened. He also stated that they didn't know he was going there to shoot the old man. He was then asked, what did the three of them do after they left the Chatsworth's residence. He said that Joker drove around for a while and just kept saying, 'He should've given me what's mine'.

"By that time, they had really become worried and scared because of not knowing what he was going to do next and he was acting like a wild man. They finally ended up at a local bar by the pier where they sometimes went. He said they were there about an hour when Sinclaire told them, 'Let's go'. He said they started walking down towards the pier and his guess was Stevenson had begun to have enough because he asked Joker, 'Why did he have to shoot that old man?' Joker looked at him and said, 'He brought it on himself; he should've given me the money.'

"At that point, Bishop said he could tell Stevenson was really getting scared because he told Joker, 'Now you're going to have the cops looking for us because you went crazy and still didn't get any money'. Then he told Joker, 'You two can do whatever you want, but I'm leaving'.

"Joker wouldn't hear of it and told Stevenson that, 'Nobody was getting out'. That's when he pulled out the gun and shot Stevenson. When he turned to run away, he shot him again in the back. He said by that time he was too scared to say anything because Sinclaire was laughing like crazy.

"He was asked what they did after Stevenson was shot. He said he didn't do anything, he was so scared that he guesses he froze because the next thing he knew, Sinclaire was yanking him by the arm saying, 'Let's get out of here', and started running. He didn't care where to just as long as it was away from there and poor Stevenson.

"He was then asked, 'Whose idea was it to carjack the man at the service station?' He said, 'It is Joker's idea'. He said there was no way that they could go back to his car because the cops would be looking for it and they needed a ride to get out of there."

Det. Hauser said, "Guys, that kid had a remorseful look on his face as he said he thought maybe Joker was looking for a car someplace to just 'hot-wire' and drive off. It never occurred to him that he was planning all along to carjack somebody. When they arrived at the service station, Joker looked around and there was no one outside but this old man who was just getting into his car. Before he could think about it, Joker started running up to the car, snatching the old man out and throwing him to the ground while holding the gun to his head. He thought Joker was going to shoot the old man and he believes that, if the man had tried to put up a fight, he would have shot him too. He stated that he felt sorry for the man and that he was becoming sick to his stomach.

"He was asked, 'What happened after that?' He said, 'Joker jumped into the car yelling, "Hurry up and get in the car, stupid"'.

"He was asked, 'What did you do then?' He said, 'I did what I was told to do and got into the car; he was still holding the gun'.

"'Where did you and Joker go after leaving the service station?' he was asked. He said, 'We had to get out of the area fast, so we jumped on the 101 freeway'.

"He said that he asked Joker where they were going because the cops were going to be looking for the car. He said Joker laughed and said he knew of a place where they wouldn't be looking for them.

"He was then asked, 'Where is this place?' He gazed at me hard for a few seconds and said, "Look, Detective, Joker has hurt people. I don't want to be responsible for hurting anyone especially, since they had nothing to do with what he did. I told him whether he believed me or not; it was entirely up to him, but we're not out to hurt anyone. We're just trying to get to the bottom of the situation"'."

"It was obvious that he was becoming nervous. After a few seconds had passed, he said, "They went to Sinclaire's cousin's house in Arleta."

At that instant, Maxwell and Skylar looked at each other, and in unison, they asked Det. Hauser, "Did you just say Arleta?"

Puzzled, he stared at the both of them and replied, "Yes, what is it?"

Skylar was the first to speak saying, "The Arleta Police Department contacted us here stating that the owner of a car wash business reported to have found an abandoned car when he went to open for business. He gave the make of the car and the license plate number. After running the plates through, they discovered that it was the car taken in a carjacking incident in this area the day before. You also stated that Bishop told you that he and Joker went to a cousin's house there, am I correct?" he asked Hauser.

"Yes, that's absolutely correct."

Maxwell said, "Well, there are no records stating that Joker has any known relatives."

However, neither Skylar nor Maxwell acknowledged to Hauser that they were aware of the relationship between Chatsworth and Joker, so they allowed him to continue.

"I told him there was nothing in Joker's records stating that he has any relatives anywhere. Then he said that he didn't think he had any kin either because he never spoke about it. However, when they finally made it there, he learned that not only did he have a cousin, he also has an uncle the one he shot, Steven Chatsworth. I asked him, 'What!' He said, 'Yeah, that's right, Mr. Chatsworth is Joker's blood uncle'."

Maxwell and Skylar gazed at each for a brief second, then back at Hauser. Bishop stated that during their conversation, while they were there is when he learned the truth. Then Hauser looked at them and said, "I told you guys this case has more twists in it than a maze. I asked him, what is the cousin's name? At first, he was somewhat hesitant, then he said Joker only introduced him to me as John D. I asked him what happened while the two of them were there. Suddenly, there was a composed expression on his face when he said, 'They were only there until it was dark', but just long enough for him to learn about Joker and Chatsworth. He stated that he could tell Joker was becoming anxious to leave anyway. I asked him why he said that. He said because he didn't like what John D. was saying and he was the only man that he'd ever seen stand up to him. Bishop said when he first saw John D., he thought to himself he was as loony as Joker, but other than their physical appearances, there was no similarity between the two. I asked him just what was he saying. He said, 'They resemble identical twins, but John D. is more serious and open spoken'. He didn't care for the predicament that Joker had gotten himself into and he straight out told him so. Then he said, 'That's when everything came out'. I asked him what he meant by 'everything'. He said, 'When Joker told John D. that there's only one other person out there who knows about him and he's in the hospital, that's when he began to wonder to himself because the only person in the hospital that he knew of was Mr. Chatsworth, but how could he possibly know about John D.?' He said the big shocker came when John D. asked Joker, 'Just what did happen between you and Mr. Chatsworth?' Joker told him that Mr. Chatsworth had him do all of his dirty work and when it became too hot, he fired him. That's when John D. told Joker, 'He couldn't fire him because he wasn't just someone who was working for him'. He asked Joker, 'Is that what the shooting was about?' Det. Hauser said he asked Bishop, 'What was the shooting about?' He said Joker stated the shooting wasn't about his trying to fire him because he knew he couldn't. Mr. Chatsworth told him to leave and not come back, then he said he didn't care about that, but he wanted everything that was his, and when he told Mr. Chatsworth that, he refused. Bishop said Joker told John D. that he went back for him to release his inheritance, and when he flatly told him to get out, that's when he just lost it and shot him. Det.

Hauser said he asked Bishop, 'Are you saying that Joker shot Chatsworth over his inheritance?' He said, 'Yes, but we—that is, Stevenson and I— didn't know anything about an inheritance at the time of the shooting'. Det. Hauser said, 'So, the motive for his shooting Chatsworth is the inheritance'. Bishop said, 'During their conversation, John D. told Joker he was sorry it had come to that; there should have been some way for him to reason with Chatsworth, and said after all, he is your uncle'. Bishop said at that point he was becoming loose at the end because he finally realized why Joker was always trying to put him and Stevenson down, but he's the one who's nuts. He said John D. gave Joker a hard look and told him, 'You're lucky the old man's not dead, and let's face it, he is your legal guardian; that's the way your folks had it set up'. Then he said, 'What I don't understand, though, is why Mr. Chatsworth didn't release the money last year when he reached age twenty-five?' Joker asked him, 'Why did your parents choose your uncle anyway, because for as long as he could remember he'd always been a stickler for perfection?' In addition, according to Bishop, John D. told Joker that he probably wasn't going to like what he was about to say, but he was going to tell him anyway and he did! He told him that he didn't believe anyone else wanted the responsibility of having to deal with him. Even his parents said he was irresponsible because, to him, everything was a joke. He said Joker was spoiled rotten and as a result, they were always bailing him out of one incident or another because he pulled those stupid pranks on people and laughed it off as a joke. Bishop said, 'That's when he thought to himself, so that's why he's called Joker'. Even then, he said, 'But nobody was seriously hurt by it'. The next time John D. spoke, his tone was much different; in fact, he said it was rough. He told Joker, 'That's the point, because no one was hurt you just thought it was all right to continue doing it. You're lucky that no one was injured because you would have been in a world of trouble. It's time for you to grow up and assume responsibility for your own actions. Then he asked Joker, if had it ever occurred to him that the old man, Mr. Chatsworth, didn't believe he was ready to receive the inheritance yet. Then Joker asked him, 'What was I supposed to do?' John D. told him that he was in a lot of trouble and the only one who could straighten it out was himself, and for once in his life, he should think about it! Suddenly Bishop said, 'All the while John D. was talking, he was looking at Joker. He wasn't hearing what his cousin was saying, only the fastest way out there was the only thing on his mind.

"Det. Hauser said, 'I asked Bishop what he and Joker did after his cousin had finished talking to him?' He said, 'By that time, it was dark'.

They had to get out of there fast before John D.'s wife got home. He gathered she didn't care very much for Joker because he'd already told Joker that if she came home and saw them, there would be the devil to pay! Joker just told him that they were leaving before she got there. Det. Hauser said he asked Bishop where he went after leaving John D.'s house. He said Joker drove around until he spotted the car wash that was closed. Joker said that was a good place to leave the car because it wouldn't be open until the next morning. Besides, there was a rest area not far from there. They made their way to it and just as they arrived there, some kind of poultry truck was about to pull out. Joker stopped the man and paid him fifty dollars to let them ride in the back of the truck. At first, he stared at them somewhat funnily, but when he looked at the money, he shrugged his shoulders, unlocked the door, and told them to get in. I began to laugh and said, 'So that's why the two of you smell like a poultry farm?' He lowered his head and sheepishly replied, 'Yes'. I asked him where they went after that. Bishop said they got off the truck near the Santa Monica freeway off-ramp and hitched a ride to the construction company where they used to hang out, the one Joker stole the dump truck from. I told him, 'You know aiding and abetting fugitives from justice is considered a criminal offense. However, according to what he had stated regarding John D., he appears to be a man who strongly believes in fair play, and he has provided us with some valuable information. Since the two of them didn't remain there and he assisted them in no way in avoiding the authorities, in the interest of justice I can't think of any reason why it would be necessary to bring him into this. We have what we need, and I believe in this case, we can just say he was unfortunate.

"Enough to have been caught up in a bad situation. We were nearly done when I told him that I was quite curious about something. I told him there's no record of his ever having been involved with the law, that is, until now. How and why did he become involved with Sinclaire in the first place? Guys, the kid looked directly into my eyes and said, 'I've wished many times over that I'd never set eyes on him. Stevenson and I were looking for employment and we met him at one of the local bars where we used to just hang out. After going there a few times, one day Joker told us that he could get us a job making good money working for Mr. Chatsworth. At the time, we had no idea that he was nuts until we began seeing some of the crazy pranks he was always playing on people. In addition, the strangest thing about it though, he laughed it off as a joke and seemed to have thrived on it. Oh, we thought about leaving a couple of times, but Mr. Chatsworth paid us good money, so we just stayed. Then he had a remorseful expression on his face when he said, 'If we had left, maybe Stevenson would still be alive'. After that, I told him we were done, and thanked him for his cooperation. He just looked at me and said, 'You're welcome, Detective Hauser'."

Maxwell listened intensely as Det. Hauser gave an account of the interrogation, which confirmed the information that Atkins had conveyed to him earlier, specifically, in reference to the relationship between Chatsworth and the suspect, Freddy Sinclaire.

Skylar said, "Well, there's no more speculation regarding motives for both shootings. Det. Hauser, what about Sinclaire? As far as you're aware, has any progress been made towards getting anything significant out of him?"

He stared at Skylar, laughed, and asked, "Is that just wishful thinking, Detective Skylar? From all indications, it appears that he's going to be transferred to the psycho ward until the court hearing. You know something has me puzzled—why has Mr. Chatsworth chosen to keep the relationship between him and Joker a secret all of this time?"

Skylar said, "Man, I can't answer that question. I don't understand either."

Maxwell said, "Perhaps we'll have the answers to a number of questions when he's well enough to receive visitors if he doesn't have a relapse first. You know, this whole episode has been in the news and if I'm any judge of character at this point, Steven Chatsworth is anything but calm."

Det. Hauser directed his attention to Maxwell and asked, "Incidentally, during Bishop's interrogation he stated that Chatsworth fired the three of them after talking with a private investigator who had come to his home. He also said that Joker told his cousin that he had been doing all of his dirty work and when it got too hot for him, that's when he told them to get out. I didn't understand what that part was about, so I asked Bishop what he meant. He said that Chatsworth had them do some things that were not right, but he didn't elaborate on it so we just proceeded with the questioning."

Skylar looked at Maxwell, then Hauser, and said, "Detective, that is another part of this maze. Maxwell is doing some investigation that involves Steven Chatsworth and he's the private investigator who was at Chatsworth's residence the day of the firing."

Det. Hauser stared at each of them and said, "This situation is like a revolving door. Well, I'm finished for now, I have a lot of paperwork to get out. Thanks for the company, gentlemen. He looked at Skylar, smiled and said, "Unfortunately, I'm still on duty."

After Det. Hauser had gone, Skylar gazed at Maxwell and said, "You know, this Chatsworth case is becoming more complex by the minute. Now I'm curious to learn exactly where this John D. fellow fit into all of this and what relation he is to Chatsworth. Now we know why the car was found abandoned in Arleta. Maxwell, I wonder just what other secrets Steven Chatsworth's closet conceals?"

As if to be staring into space and then focusing his eyes directly on Skylar, he slowly said, "I don't know, Skylar, but you can rest assured

I'm going to find out and soon." He spoke without reservation and Skylar knew he was determined to do just that!

Maxwell smiled and said, "Now getting back to my question before we were interrupted, what are you going to do next, Detective?"

"I'm a crime investigator, remember?" he asked, returning the smile. "Oh, by the way, the W.C. wants to see you in his office." "Oh, I wonder what that's about," he said to Skylar.

"I would say there's one way to find out, wouldn't you?"

"Right, you are. When is he in his office?"

Looking at his wristwatch, Skylar said, "As a matter of fact, he's there now. This week he's scheduled for the day shift. Incidentally, Bradford, what about your case now?"

"Well, that depends on a number of things, Jacob. As you know, there are still some unanswered questions pertaining to Chatsworth that need to be clarified before I can bring the situation to a resolution. In addition, from all indications, I'd say the case is far from being resolved. I haven't checked in with Blake Colwell yet, but I believe the owner, Claudia Carrington, should have returned from her trip abroad by this time. At that moment, Maxwell's cell phone rang. He checked the number, looked at Skylar, and with a broad smile on his face said, "Hello, Blake, what a surprise. I had planned to call you later this morning. You sound awful; what's the problem?"

"Chatsworth telephoned you a while ago—what did he say? Oh, oh I knew he was going to hit the ceiling when the news came out. Well, I'm in the process of taking care of something and when I'm finished, I'll give you a call."

He gazed at Skylar, laughed, and said, "As you heard. That was Blake Colwell informing me that Chatsworth telephoned him ranting about the incident at his home, and get this, his condition has improved, and his physicians are allowing him to have visitors now. That, my friend, is the break I've been waiting for. He said, however, there was another problem in the situation. Claudia isn't aware that Chatsworth and her own husband is responsible for the business scandal that developed. What?" Jacob asked.

"Yes, that's right. Chatsworth masterminded the whole situation with a little assistance from Charles, who was just a ploy in his diabolical scheme to ruin the firm." This time, it was Jacob who leaned back, and gazing directly into Bradford's eyes, said, "Good grief, man. He then asked Bradford why he would want to ruin the business." "It was a vendetta, Jacob," he told him.

"Against whom, for crying out loud?"

"Would you believe David Lansing himself?"

"But the man's dead so what could he possibly expect to accomplish?"

"Listen, my friend, first you'd have to understand this man's way of thinking. In his eyes, the firm was representative of Lansing. He point blank told me that he had only two regrets. When I asked what they might be, guess what his reply was."

"I can't begin to imagine."

"One, Claudia is caught in the middle of it all, and two, Lansing isn't alive to witness it happening."

Skylar gazed at him for a time, then said, "He didn't succeed because you came on the scene."

"Precisely! Bradford, I would say he had a grudge."

"It was more than that. It was something that had been festering in him for many years."

"How does he live with that kind of hatred?" Skylar asked him.

"It appears that some people thrive off it."

"Maybe, but for myself, I can't imagine ever living like that."

"Neither can I, Jacob."

"Well, the breakfast was great and thanks for the treat. The next time, it's on me."

"You got it, Bradford." They both smiled at each other fondly; a common bond had formed between them that wasn't there before.

Bradford said, "I'm headed for the station, enjoy your day off."

"I plan to do just that, believe me, by going surfing," Jacob said smiling.

Bradford's inner thought was, I was correct; he is a surfer.

Atkins sat slowly and deliberately back down in his chair never shifting his focus off Chatsworth and gazing into his eyes. He said, "Steven Chatsworth, we've known each other for a great many years. I've always assumed we were more than attorney and client, but friends. How could you of all people be this deceptive with me?"

Chatsworth lifted his head and stared out the window for a few seconds, then looking into Atkins' eyes he saw the hurt and perhaps disappointment in them. That obviously stirred something within him that he thought was completely lost. He stared directly into his eyes and said "Victor, it happened years ago. A young woman and I were attending college together. It began with occasional dates, then we began seeing each other more frequently. About a year later, we both realized that we were in love with each other, but there was a problem. While I was struggling my way through college, her folks were taking expensive trips abroad. For some time, they didn't know about us because we both resided on campus. Her major was horticulture and of course, mine was structural engineering. She and I had discussed getting married after graduating college, but her parents learned of our relationship and didn't approve of it. One day, we were out on an excursion, and she said there was something that she wanted to tell me. About three or four weeks later, she asked me to meet her at the little restaurant that we often went to up from campus, and of course; I told her that I would meet her after my last class session. I knew something wasn't just right because after her parents' last trip abroad about two weeks prior to that she didn't appear to be as happy as she had been. I asked her if something was wrong. She just looked at me and her eyes began to swell with tears. She said, 'Steven, my parents don't want us to see each other anymore'. I asked if they had given her an explanation as to why. She started to cry and said after college, they wanted her to marry one of her father's friend's sons who had just graduated from medical school. Naturally, I said, 'What?!' Then she told me that she loved me and always would. That night, we stayed off campus and went to the motel. We saw each other for about two months after that night. One day when I telephoned her dorm, I was informed that her parents had checked her out and she was gone. I called her home and each time I asked to speak with her I was told that she wasn't there. I got fed up with it, so one day I drove out there, which was about two weeks later. That's when I got the shock of my young life. Victor, they had moved lock, stock, and barrel. I was devastated at the prospect of not ever seeing her again. I tried contacting her in every way I possibly could but always came up with nothing. Then one day, just before graduating I received a message that I had a visitor waiting in the lobby. I didn't know who it was or what to expect. As I entered the lobby, I saw this handsomely dressed, tall slender woman with salt and pepper hair. Her smile was warm and captivating as she looked at me. She introduced herself to me and said she was Cynthia's aunt. Man, you could have blown me over with a feather. As I sat in a chair directly facing her she said, 'I'm here on behalf of my niece and your son'. She undoubtedly thought I was going to collapse because she began to laugh and I suddenly realized that my mouth was wide open and her laughter was the same as Cynthia's. After quickly gaining control of myself, I asked her, 'You did say Cynthia and my son?' She laughed again and said, 'Yes, Steven. I regret to say that I'm the bearer of both sad and good news. My niece passed away last year. She died of pneumonia and complications, but before she died, I had to make her a promise that I would raise John D. and try to find you, and of course, give you the explanation that she could not.

"Victor, as this strange woman sat there speaking to me in her soft voice, all I could think about was Cynthia and remember how much we loved each other. Then it dawned on me that she'd said I had, or shall I say *have*, a son. She explained that when her parents learned of her pregnancy, that is when they took her out of school and moved out of the state forbidding her to ever contact you again. They became furious with her because she refused to consent to a marriage with someone whom she didn't love, and she became pregnant to boot. However, they did allow her to keep her baby. He was her pride and joy in life, and you remained the love of her life. She also told me that she never had the opportunity to tell you that you were going to be a father. In fact, she didn't know herself until much later. She did return to school and received her degree in horticulture. Her parents moved abroad, she and your son came to live with me. Steven, he was my brother, but they were wrong, and I told them so. She had the right to choose her own path in life without any interference from them.

"I respected this woman and admired her for her courage. After she'd finished speaking, I asked her where my son was. She told me that he was at her home being cared for by her housekeeper while she was with me, and would I care to see him. I told her that I certainly would. She gave me the address and directions for getting there. Two days later, I saw my son for the first time, and I couldn't hold back the tears because he had his mother's smile and her eyes. I remained there for two days because it was time for graduation and I had to get back, but I definitely wanted to stay longer. After getting my degree, I went to work for a large construction company. I sent them a check each month and every two weeks I went to visit them."

Suddenly, a deep sadness fell upon his face when he said she passed away during his freshman year in college. Victor gazed at him and asked, "How was your relationship with him, Steven?"

He thought for a moment and said, "You know, it's strange that you should ask me that question."

Victor asked him, "Why is it strange?"

He responded, "Because lying here in the hospital I suddenly realized that I alienated my own son, the same way his grandparents did his mother."

Victor stared at him and recognized the sadness that appeared in his eyes and asked, "What did you do, Steven?"

"I wanted him to complete college, but in his junior year, he chose to enlist in the military instead. He was there for four years and during that time, we didn't communicate that often. You didn't mention it, but I saw the news and how that lunatic nephew of mine wrecked my home. I can't imagine what he thought he was doing because all he did was compile the charges that are already pending against him. I'll tell you this—where he's going, maybe they will give him the medical help that he needs. Now this incident with Freddy, I feel that I should've shown more interest in my own son. He has a stubborn streak just like his old man so I'm making the first move and can only hope it's not too late. I would like to know whenever I do start having grandchildren," he said with a smile. Finally, he said, "I apologize for not having confided in you earlier, Victor. I ask if you can forgive me."

"Of course, I forgive you, Steven, I believe you've learned your lesson now," he said smiling. "Incidentally, how long has it been since you last spoke with your son?"

"Around a month ago, I believe."

"All right, Steven, I'll see what I can do."

"Thank you, Victor."

"You're welcome."

Just as he entered through the front door of the police station, the W.C. was coming toward the front desk. He looked in Maxwell's direction and said, "You finally made it, I see."

"Yes, I understand you want to have a talk with me."

"That's correct. Will you accompany me back to my office please?"

"Yes, of course." After closing the door behind them, he said, "Maxwell, first I'd like to congratulate you on your assistance in the apprehension of those two suspects. Without your information, I'm afraid the time span of our catching them would have been much greater."

He smiled and said, "I'm glad that I was able to help." Leaning back in his chair while focusing his eyes on him, he said, "Maxwell, I'm very much aware of your background and your reputation. We can utilize your type of expertise in this department, you're still well within the age guideline to come in and you have the training."

He smiled at him and said, "Thanks for the consideration, but I enjoy what I'm doing and I'm in no way constrained. This way I'm not under orders and I'm my own boss."

"Well, I can certainly appreciate that fact and your honesty. Oh, by the way, I paid a visit to Chatsworth at the hospital, and he asked me if I would give you a message."

"Oh?"

"Yes, he said something quite strange, and I still don't understand for the life of me what he meant!"

"What was that, if I might ask?"

"After I explained everything to him including your participation, he said, 'I knew Maxwell was going to be trouble from the first time I saw him!' Then he said, 'We have something to settle, would you ask him to

come to the hospital at his earliest convenience?'"

Maxwell grinned and asked, "Oh, he did, did he?"

"Well, this is certainly good news. And I most definitely will answer his request."

Now standing and smiling, he said, "Thank you, Commander, for your interest and the message."

"You're welcome, Maxwell, and if you should ever need this department's assistance in any way, please don't hesitate to let us know.

I'm glad to have met you. Again, thank you."

"The same here, Commander," he responded with a broad smile.

"Mr. Colwell, Mr. Maxwell is on the line, sir."

"Thank you, Jenny. Please put him through."

"Hello, Brad, I'm pleased you called, Claudia is back home and she's aware of the incident involving Chatsworth. She's coming here to the office for all of the details, but what are we going to tell her about the situation since both Chatsworth and Charles were involved?"

He said, "Blake, I understand your concern. We're going to have to inform her eventually, but I was hoping to get the opportunity to speak with Chatsworth first. There are a number of things that he'll have to clarify because since the incident with Joker occurred there have been new developments in this bizarre situation. I can't resolve it until everything has been cleared up and there are no more open holes."

"You're correct and I certainly agree with you. How are things with the department?"

"Oh, things are just fine, Blake. Would you believe I was asked to consider coming on the force?"

"I would most certainly have been disappointed if they didn't ask you. You have the training and the experience, you know."

"Look, you old fox, you of all people know that's why I resigned from the military, because of constraint. This way, I'm not under from anyone and I'm my own boss."

"Yes, I know, buddy. Well, what have you got new this time? Not another stolen dump truck I hope!"

"No, not this time," he said laughing. "However, it does appear that since the incident with Chatsworth and his men has been resolved by the authorities, I was given a message that he wants me to visit him at the hospital. His words were, 'We have something to settle'. Blake, this is the opportunity I've been anxiously waiting for. Perhaps we can get the situation with the firm resolved finally."

"You want me to come with you, am I correct?"

"Yes, you're the attorney for the firm and I'm the investigator hired to search out the truth and bring a resolve. However, I can't do this until I know what his position is going to be in the matter before speaking with Claudia."

"Brad, you've got a very logical point there and I agree with you. When do you want to visit him?"

"When is it convenient for you?"

"The only thing that is scheduled for today is Claudia's visit at two-thirty this afternoon."

"It's one o'clock now; this should give us enough time to visit him and return to your office before she arrives."

"Mr. Chatsworth, you have two more visitors, sir."

"Good, send them in nurse, please."

Blake entered the room first, followed by Maxwell. There were two other people who were also present in the room—they recognized Atkins, but not the young man who was sitting beside Chatsworth's bed. As they approached, Maxwell stopped in his tracks, thinking no, this can't be, Joker's locked up, I'm certain of it. Suddenly, he remembered the description of Joker's cousin that Bishop had given Det. Hauser.

They acknowledged the other men, and then Blake turned his attention to Chatsworth and asked, "Hello, Steven, how are you feeling?"

Staring at Blake, then Maxwell, he replied, "I've certainly felt better, Blake, but thanks for asking." Then turning his attention to Maxwell, he said, "Maxwell, I see you received my message."

"Yes, I did, Chatsworth." Gazing steadily at him, Maxwell asked, "What is it that you would like to settle?"

He replied, "First before we begin, I'd like to introduce my son, John D. Chatsworth. Bradford and Blake stared at each other, Atkins, John D., and back to Chatsworth. Then suddenly, they all began to laugh because of their facial expressions.

Atkins said, "You should've seen my face when he first told me."

Blake said, "I've known you for many years, Steven, and I realize you're a very personal and complicated man to understand, but you've never so much as indicated that you have a son."

He looked directly into Blake's eyes and said, "Nor did I acknowledge that Freddy is my nephew. You know, lying here in this bed gave me a chance to look at things as they really are and to put them in their perspective order. Perhaps the shooting incident was a wake-up call to reality for me...I believe so anyway." Turning his attention to Maxwell, he said, "Maxwell, I realize you've probably got a few questions to ask me.

But first, there are two main issues to settle with you."

"And what might they be, pray to tell?"

Chatsworth repositioned himself in the hospital bed, then spoke and said, "Number one, I haven't changed my mind about you. I knew you were going to be in trouble from the first time I saw you."

He smiled and asked, "What is issue number two?"

"I was given detailed information on what you did and I never thought the day would come when I'd say this, but I'm saying it now and I don't say anything that I don't mean." Then, unexpectedly to everyone including Maxwell, he extended his hand and said, "I thank you for the courage in what you did, Maxwell."

He shook his hand and said, "You're more than welcome."

Chatsworth's gesture brought smiles to everyone's faces and even his own. With a broad grin, Maxwell asked him, "Do you recall when I told you that I'm an individualist?"

He replied, "Yes, I do, and I must admit you are, Maxwell." Then he gazed at him for a second or two before saying, "I'm quite curious about a number of things, Maxwell. Tell me, how did you know that the shooting at my residence wasn't the result of the firing?"

He said, "To begin with, he didn't try to kill you because he very well could have. Then I began to question why they returned to your residence after you'd ordered them off your property. At that time, as you were speaking, I observed each of their faces and Joker had a sneaky grin on his face. I felt very strongly that he was going to be up to something sinister. Whatever the reason, it had to be very important to him and when he didn't succeed in getting what he wanted he just went crazy and started shooting. There's also your housekeeper's statement to the authorities. She stated that she heard you tell the man to get out and he told you he wanted everything that belonged to him then. From the beginning, there was speculation of his having been fired as being the motive for the shooting, but I just couldn't accept that; I knew there had to be something else involved. Your housekeeper's statement only confirmed my suspicion. The next thing was what provoked him into killing Stevenson, one of the men who was always with him. That's when I began inquiring about him because, at that point, he had gone wild with the second shooting. After that was the carjacking incident, which was his sure way of getting out of the area as fast as they could. I knew he wasn't going to come here; he was wild, not stupid, and he was too busy eluding the authorities until he could put his plan into action, whatever it was. When Atkins and I met, that's when I realized that his motive for shooting you was the inheritance and, of course, he is your nephew. There was no knowledge of your son until after they were apprehended. When the authorities found the car taken during the carjacking abandoned in Arleta, I first believed he was leaving a false trail to throw the authorities off track. That is until the interrogating officer in charge of the case gave an account of Bishop's statement. That's when I realized he had gone there to assimilate his plan without having to worry about the authorities because no one knew of John D.'s existence. I had a gut feeling that he was planning to do something else, but I couldn't be specific as to what and that became an annoyance to me. I decided to visit one of the construction sites and while I was there, a call came in that Joker and Bishop had been seen getting off a truck near the Santa Monica freeway off-ramp, which meant they had eluded the authorities again and returned to this area. After leaving there, I went to another construction company and just missed them according to the foreman. They had hitched a ride there and were trying to get someone to loan them a car. He stated that Joker was raving and ranting that you owed him a lot of money and he was going to collect. I reminded him that you are in the hospital so how had he planned to collect anything? He stated that he didn't know and didn't ask, because they just wanted them to leave. While we were talking, one of the drivers came yelling and asking for the boss. The foreman and I stared at each other because, at that time, we had no way of knowing why he was so excited. Until the owner and he came out of his office screaming that Joker and his imbecile friend had stolen his dump truck."

At that revelation, everyone in the room began to laugh. Maxwell said, "I asked them, how could they have taken a big dump truck out of there and no one saw them leave? The foreman said, 'They have trucks coming in and going out through the day so no one really paid any attention. Besides, who would expect them to take a big dump truck?' I told him that it was probably best that no one did catch them, because they could have become another victim. That is when it dawned on me what he was planning to do. He didn't care about the damage he was going to do to your residence. I immediately alerted the authorities and informed them of what had transpired and my assessment of the whole situation. I'm only sorry there was no advanced indication of what he was actually going to do."

Chatsworth gazed hard at him, smiled, and said, "Had it not been for your persistence in the matter, I'm afraid things would have been much worse, so don't allow it to disturb you further." He smiled and said, "Now, Maxwell, I understand why you have the reputation for being a 'nonsense man'. He said, no one knew of my relationship with Freddy because I didn't want him to go about boasting especially, to the other men. That is why I made no distinction in them."

Maxwell said, "Now I understand your position in that area, and you've answered the question." As if to be thinking, he suddenly turned his attention to Blake Colwell and said, "You're the firm's attorney and you know there was an agreement between Lansing and me years ago, as I would become the silent partner in the firm. I believe these are the papers that you were holding over his head when you threatened him prior to Claudia's marriage."

Both Blake and Bradford stared at him in total surprise. Chatsworth smiled at him and said, "Yes, Blake, I know all about it. Lansing told me about the threat that you had made. Claudia isn't aware of it, nor was Claudette. That young lady has suffered enough because of something she had nothing to do with. I really don't know how you're going to solve the problem with that idiot husband of hers, but I'm officially terminating my partnership from the firm, effective as of today Blake, and you may destroy those papers that are in your files thereby, drawing a stare from Bradford.

Staring directly into his eyes and with a broad smile he said, "Incidentally, Chatsworth, the next time we meet I hope it will be under a different circumstance."

Looking at him with a return smile, Chatsworth said, "I believe I'd like that, Maxwell."

After leaving the hospital, Blake and Bradford headed for Blake's office for the meeting with Claudia. It was two-fifteen p.m. The lengthy meeting with Chatsworth had thrown them off schedule. There was just barely enough time for them to discuss the situation between themselves before her arrival because she believed in punctuality. Blake's inner concern was Claudia's reaction regarding everything, including Chatsworth and Charles's involvement in the whole nasty mess. Bradford's thoughts were of Chatsworth and he wondered what actually influenced his decision to terminate the partnership. Then he recalled the old adage that, "A leopard doesn't change his spots." However, in Chatsworth's case, he might have to disagree with that to a certain extent.

The both of them arrived at Blake's office about the same time, and taking a brief look at his wristwatch, Blake said, "We have just enough time to discuss this before she arrives."

Bradford stared at him and saw the concern on Blake's face and his instincts returned once again which led him back to his first observation. Blake was definitely concealing something from him and why was he so protective of Claudia? Oh well, first things first. The present situation had priority over his instincts. Blake informed Jenny to send Claudia in as soon as she arrived and to hold all his calls. He and Bradford went into his office to discuss the situation. Claudia arrived punctually at two-thirty p.m. and upon entering Blake's office she was greeted by both Blake and Bradford. After they were seated, Blake began by saying, "Claudia, my dear, I believe we can finally bring this situation with the firm to closure."

"Now, this is what I consider to be a wonderful homecoming present," she said smiling.

"Bradford is going to bring you up to date with a detailed report of his investigation and the findings."

She stared at them and said, "First, I would like to know what has happened during my absence. I saw the early morning news and Chatsworth's home looked as if a tornado had gone through there and they showed a big dump truck stuck inside of it."

They glanced at each other. Blake hunched his shoulder and nodded his head as if to say, you might as well tell her.

Bradford said, "Claudia, while you were absent Chatsworth was shot by his nephew."

She stared at him and asked, "Did you just say his nephew, Brad?"

"Yes, I did. You see, according to Chatsworth's explanation as to why no one knew of their relationship, he didn't want him boasting to the other men who worked for him. Therefore, as far as they and everyone else were aware, he was another employee. Chatsworth is the legal guardian over his inheritance. They disobeyed an order he'd given, so he fired them and told them to stay away. They went back to his residence. Apparently, Joker (the nephew) decided that since he'd been fired he wanted his inheritance and when he asked Chatsworth for it he refused. That's when Joker went wild with anger and shot him. He is the one who was shot by the authorities."

She asked him, "Why did he drive the dump truck into the residence?"

"He was completely out of control and my guess is he didn't care how much damage was incurred. Bishop, the other suspect, said when he last saw him he was attempting to get into the safe, yelling, 'I want all of my money'."

"How is Chatsworth doing now?" she asked him.

"Oh, he's improving, in fact, quite well."

Bradford said, "Claudia, as you know, I was hired to search out the truth and bring an early resolve. The investigation was more extensive and complex than both Blake and I had anticipated because we were expecting to find the allegations made against the firm to have been false. After all of the inquiries and close observations, I had to conclude that they were valid. Claudia, do you recall our conversation when we first met and I told you that I was going to go deeper inside the firm?"

"Yes, Brad, I do recall your words and I told you to go ahead with the investigation; I wouldn't interfere in any way."

He said, "Every turn I made led me directly back to the firm itself. That's when I became certain the trouble was coming from within. A number of people were directly and some indirectly involved in the scandal and, unfortunately, not all of them were by choice—"

She interrupted and asked him, "What do you mean, Brad, they were not all by choice?"

"Well, let's just say most of them were being used as pawns in a ploy to divert attention away from the true motives."

Curiously staring at him, she asked, "And just what were the true motives, Brad?"

He said, "To seek control of the firm, and to completely ruin it."

She looked at Blake and back to him, then exclaimed, "What?!"

He sat back, crossing his legs, and gazing directly into her eyes said, "That's right—control and to ruin the firm, Claudia."

She asked him, "But by whom and why Brad?"

He looked at Blake, who nodded his head in agreement to tell her all of it. "Chatsworth and your husband were behind the whole business scandal. As a matter of fact, they were the ones who were directly responsible for it in the first place."

She stared at the both of them in total bewilderment and asked, "Charles and Chatsworth together, why?"

"Claudia, do you recall telling Blake that during your confrontation with Charles in your home, he told you that soon he would be in control?" "Yes, I remember."

"Well, that was one of the things he was speaking of because, in fact, that was precisely what he wanted to do. First, he had to get Blake out of the way and then he'd have no problem in coercing you into giving him the control he was seeking."

She asked him, "What was Chatsworth's interest in it, and why?"

"Claudia, his was for an entirely different rationale. To begin with, from the information Chatsworth gave me, Charles went to him. Apparently, he was disgruntled by the fact that your father had minimized his authority in the firm. Since they're gone and Blake's no longer in the picture that would leave no one but him. What better way to gain an ally than to have someone who had no vested interest in the firm. Number one, what dear Charles didn't know was the man whom he'd gone to assist him in his little scheme was the opportunity he'd been seeking for years. Number two, neither did he know that Chatsworth was a silent partner in the firm."

Upon hearing that statement, Claudia sat directly up in her chair, looked at both Bradford and Blake in wild astonishment and asked Bradford, "Am I hearing you correctly?"

"I'm afraid you are, Claudia. Chatsworth was your father's silent partner long before you were born."

She stared at Blake with questioning eyes and asked him, "Blake, did you know about this?"

He replied, "Yes, I did, Claudia. However, I was not aware of it when I first came to the firm, but learned of it later. Since I'm the firm's attorney, I suppose your father thought I should at least know about that! The agreement was made between the two following the firm's name changed to what it is now."

"Did my mother know about this?" she asked him.

"No, Chatsworth stated that she was never informed of the agreement between the two of them." Blake looked at her and said, "Brad and I paid a visit to Chatsworth at the hospital this afternoon, Claudia. He has terminated his partnership in the firm effective as of today."

"Oh, he has, has he?" she asked in a tone that was completely unlike her.

Blake replied, "Yes, he has, Claudia."

She looked away for a moment or two, then asked, "Why the sudden change of heart, Blake, and just why was he trying to ruin the firm to begin with?"

Bradford stared at Blake and knew he was just shadowing around what was the inevitable so he began. "Claudia, for all its worth, I honestly don't believe his gesture was sudden. Chatsworth's statement to Blake and me was he feels you've suffered enough. As his rationale for wanting to ruin the firm, it had nothing whatsoever to do with you. That was something he had been contemplating for years. Charles only opened the door of opportunity for him to carry out his plan. You see, something occurred years ago that had involved your father and Chatsworth vowed to exact revenge against him for what had happened. In addition, in his eyes since your father is no longer here, the firm is representative of him and that is why he was determined to ruin it. It was no more than an illogical concept of a man with hatred in his heart."

She shifted her eyes to the floor for a few seconds, then she gazed into his eyes and while holding a steady focus asked him, "Brad, just why did

Chatsworth harbor such hatred for my father?"

He stared at her and said, "Claudia—"

She halted him before he could continue and said, "I am not a child and you don't have to protect my feelings. I want the whole truth."

His focus immediately shifted to Blake, who was apparently as shocked as he was at her question, but said nothing and just nodded his head.

Brad asked her, "Claudia, are you certain about this?"

Holding her focus on him, she said, "Yes, I'm certain!"

"According to Chatsworth's statement, it happened years ago when your father first took over the business. He had begun to take frequent trips out of the city, your mother was taking notice as well, but as far as he knew, she never said anything, at least in his presence anyway. Then one day, he received an urgent telephone call from his younger sister who lived in another city not far away. She told him it was important, and that could he come to see her. He told her yes, he would be there. When he arrived there, she explained everything to him including her pregnancy and, of course, the father's name. He was aware of the fact that he was seeing other women and so was your mother, but he said he never had the slightest indication that your father was involved with his sister. She told him that when she informed him of the pregnancy, he flatly told her to get rid of it because he wasn't going to see her anymore anyway. A few days after that, he received another telephone call informing him that his sister had committed suicide. He never said anything to your mother or your father, but vowed that one day he would make sure he paid for what he'd done. Everyone thought they were such good friends including your father. He planned it that way so no one would become suspicious of his plan."

She was quiet for a short time, then said, "This man was my father!" Her voice held a bitter connotation when she finally said, "How revolting!"

Brad looked at Blake, then said, "Claudia, I'm very sorry."

She said, "Don't be, Brad, I asked you for the truth."

Bradford said, "As for your husband's participation in all of this, that's something I'm afraid you must decide for yourself. Claudia, the job I was hired to do has finally been resolved. As of now, this case is officially closed. I have to file everything away and I'll be around for a few more days, so if you or Blake should need me for anything further, you know how you can reach me."

Claudia looked away for a moment, then said, "Blake, Brad, I asked you for the whole truth, but I had no concept that all of these things were involved. As for Charles's part in all of this, I don't know what I'm going to do at this point. I truly thank you for everything you've done and you've opened my eyes to many things." Looking directly at him, she said, "Blake, I'm going to spend a few days away to sort things out in my mind. By the time I do return, my decision will have been made."

He looked at her for a long moment and said, "Claudia, my dear, I'm truly sorry things turned out this way. Take all of the time you need."

She stood up, faced them and said, "I love the both of you and I'll let you know my decision when I return, Blake."

After Claudia departed, Blake and Bradford sat in silence for a few minutes. Neither said anything.

Finally, Blake said, "Brad, I'm quite concerned about her. She has already gone through so much now this situation with Charles isn't going to help matters any."

He looked at him and said, "Blake, she's going to make the decision that's right for her and all we can do is respect it. At this point, we don't know just what that is going to be, and frankly, neither does she. That's why she's made the choice to think about it for a while, because whatever decision she does make, I'm certain will have an everlasting effect on her life."

"You know, you just might be correct, Brad. My concern is that Charles is so unpredictable there's no way of knowing how he's going to react if her decision doesn't please him."

"Yes, that's true, but I'm afraid he'll have to reconcile himself to the fact that the ball is no longer in his court but hers this time. And his options are going to be very minimal, to say the least." Blake appeared to be mulling over that statement because he made no comment.

Bradford stood up and said, "Well, buddy, in the meanwhile, I'm going back to my office and finalizing the paperwork. This case is closed. If you should need me for anything further, you know how to reach me."

Blake stood up, walked around the desk smiling and said, "You know, Brad, a man can't ask for a stronger friendship than what we have. I thank you."

With a wide grin, he responded, "Blake, the feeling's mutual and I'll be in touch."

After Bradford's departure, Blake returned to his desk and taking Chatsworth's advice, he destroyed the agreement that had existed between him and David Lansing for over thirty years. He retrieved the letter written to him by David Lansing from his personal files. After reading through it for the second time, he reverted to the numerous speculations that Lansing had been involved in the marriage of his daughter having taken place when it did. By his own admission, the letter confirmed the speculations as having been valid. He had orchestrated the marriage between her and Charles Carrington. The motive for performing such a despicable act was unknown, but he made Charles an offer and naturally, he accepted it.

As if suddenly realizing something for the very first time, Blake thought, my gracious, Claudia wanted to know the truth, but this information is something that was totally unexpected. She's aware of Charles's involvement with Chatsworth in the business scandal, but his having conspired with David in the orchestration of their marriage is entirely different. Brad and I didn't go this far during the meeting because we—rather, I—wanted to spare her from further humiliation. But there's no way in which to determine what her reaction is going to be when she's informed that her marriage has been orchestrated by her own father from the very beginning. Speaking of "from the frying pan into the fire," he thought.

As he was leaving Blake's office, Bradford suddenly remembered that he'd promised Jacob Skylar that he would bring him up to date on the meeting with Chatsworth. Looking at his wristwatch and noting the time, he'd forgotten that Jacob was off duty. Therefore, he decided to go into his office and complete the paperwork on the business scandal and officially mark the case closed. He spent a few hours there, then decided to close shop and call it a day. He was feeling a bit tired anyway and thought a good night's rest was what he needed for a change.

After taking a ride along the oceanside, he thought it would be a good time to telephone Skylar after recalling that he had been scheduled to work the night shift. "Hello, this is Det. Jacob Skylar."

"Jacob, this is Bradford, when does your shift end?"

"Hello, Bradford, I was wondering how long I'd have to wait before hearing from you again. My shift ends in about half an hour. Where are you now?"

"I'm about two blocks away from the station."

"Good! How about our meeting at the restaurant, we can have an early lunch if that's all right with you."

"That sounds great. I've been up since dawn and I'm getting kind of hungry anyway. I'll get us a table."

"I'll see you there then. Besides, I'm anxious to learn from you how the meeting with Chatsworth went."

"Man, all I can tell you now is you've got a big surprise coming," he said laughing.

Jacob said, "Now I can hardly wait!"

As he was driving to the restaurant, Bradford's thoughts reverted to his friend, Blake Colwell. *Something's just not all together with Blake. I know he's concealing something, but the point is I can't put my finger on it right now. It's one thing to be concerned for someone, but another to become overprotective in such a way that it's beginning to affect his better judgment. From the beginning, when we spoke of Claudia, I sensed something that to me, was more than just the concern about what Charles is involved in. Now, he's becoming genuinely frustrated, and he isn't even aware of it yet.*

Bradford arrived at the restaurant and ordered coffee while awaiting Jacob's arrival. He'd consumed nearly half a cup of coffee when looking up he spotted him coming in through the front entrance.

Jacob saw him right away and walked over to their table. Seating himself, he smiled and said, "It's good to get out of there and relax for a while. Would you believe I've been busy since checking in? I didn't even get a chance to eat lunch unless you would consider a half sandwich and a glass of milk lunch."

Bradford gave him a hearty laugh and said, "Well that was something at least, which is more than I've had."

Then he smiled and said, "Let's order before we pass out, shall we?"

Jacob laughed and said, "Yes we had better because I believe we've had enough problems for a while." He signaled the waitress over to their table. Jacob ordered broiled steak, mashed potatoes, a green salad, rolls, and a slice of Angel food cake. Bradford ordered broiled chicken, rice, string beans, rolls and a slice of sweet potato pie. Their order also included milk and a fresh pot of coffee. After the waitress had taken their orders and left the table, the both of them sat back in a more relaxing position.

Skylar began by asking him, "How did your meeting with the W.C. go?"

He looked at him, smiled and said, "I think it went quite well. As a matter of fact, he tried to recruit me into the force, but you know how I feel about that! I just thanked him for the consideration and that was it. However, he told me that he'd gone to the hospital and spoke with Chatsworth and he asked him if he would give me a message. I said, 'Oh?' He said, 'Yes', and he said something quite strange that I still don't understand for the life of me what he meant. I asked him, 'What is that, if I might ask?' After he explained everything to him including my participation in the situation he said, 'I knew Maxwell was going to be trouble from the first time I saw him!' Then he said, 'We have something to settle, would you come to the hospital at your earliest convenience?' I told him that certainly was good news and I would honor his request.

"Jacob gazed at him, laughed and asked, 'So he knew you were going to be trouble from the start, huh?' Bradford smiled and said, 'So say he!' Then he said, 'After leaving the station, I telephoned Blake Colwell and gave him the news. He informed me that Claudia had returned home from her trip and saw the early morning news. She wanted to know what happened and he asked her to come to his office at two-thirty p.m. yesterday. At that time, their lunch was being served so they waited until the waitress had gone."

Then as they began to eat their meal, Bradford continued. "I explained to Blake that I believe it would be to our advantage to have a talk with Chatsworth first before meeting with Claudia because we had to know precisely what his position was going to be regarding the situation with the firm. I gave him time to get from his office and we met up at the hospital. We had just assumed that he was alone. Blake entered the room ahead of me, Jacob. Would you believe I stopped dead in my tracks?"

Jacob stared into his eyes for a couple of seconds, then he asked him, "Why did you stop, Bradford?"

"Do you recall Det? Hauser's statement when he said during the interrogation Bishop stated that Joker and his cousin could pass for identical twins. And when he was asked the cousin's last name, he didn't know it because he was introduced to him only as John D.?"

"Yes, I remember." Then Jacob said, "Wait a minute, you're not getting ready to tell me that Joker's cousin is here."

He laughed and said, "That's only half of it, my friend. Bishop's description of him was no exaggeration and when he told John D. there was only one other person who knew about him and he was in the hospital. He was referring to none other than Steven Chatsworth, whom we already knew was Joker's uncle, but what we didn't know is he's also John D.'s father."

Jacob stopped eating, gazed directly into Bradford's eyes and exclaimed, "What?!"

"He responded, 'That's right. His name is John D. Chatsworth'.

Jacob said, "So that's why they went to Arleta in the first place."

Bradford said, "Yes, and to work out his plan as to what he was going to do next."

Jacob said, "Bradford, tell me what happened next?"

"I gave him a detailed account of everything we covered. Then he asked me, 'How did you know they were going to his residence?' I told him I didn't until the dump truck came up stolen. That's when I realized that had been his plan all along. Then I alerted the authorities to inform them of what had transpired and my assessment of the whole situation. Chatsworth said that he was given detailed information on my participation in the incident. He thought the day would never come when he would say it, but he was saying it then and he never said anything that he didn't mean. Then totally unexpectedly to everyone in the room including myself, he extended his hand to me and said, 'Thank you for the courage in what you did'. Man, now that really threw me for a loop. I expressed my regret to him that there was no advanced indication of what he was going to do. He just said, 'Had it not been for your persistence in the matter, I'm afraid things would have been much worse, and you shouldn't allow it to disturb you further'. I was going to ask him why he chose to keep his relationship with Joker a secret. Before I could ask him, he said he never told anyone because he didn't want him boasting to the other men. In addition, as far as his son, I assume he feels that is a personal affair, so I never bothered to ask him."

Jacob asked him, "Brad, I know you were concerned about wrapping up your case with the firm's situation, but you were waiting to speak with Chatsworth first. Did you get anywhere?"

"As a matter of fact, Jacob, we did. He gave some information that even I wasn't aware of. He spoke directly to Blake and said since he's the firm's attorney he knew there was an agreement between he and David Lansing years ago, as he would become the silent partner in the firm. Incidentally, Jacob, this was not publicly known. He stated that he believes those are the papers that Blake was holding over Lansing's head when he threatened him prior to Claudia's marriage. I believe Blake was as surprised as I was when Chatsworth smiled at him and said he knew all about it. Lansing had told him about the threat. He said that Claudia wasn't aware of it, nor was her mother. Then he said, 'That young lady has suffered enough because of something she had nothing to do with'. He told us that he doesn't know how we're going to solve the problem with that idiot husband of hers, but he officially terminated his partnership with the firm, effective as of yesterday. In addition, Blake could destroy those papers that were in his files, which up to that time I wasn't even aware of. However, I plan to discuss that with Blake later. Before leaving I told Chatsworth the next time we meet, I hope it will be under a different circumstance. He just smiled and said he believed he'd like that!"

For a few minutes, they just sat sipping their coffee. Jacob gazed into his eyes and asked Brad, "Did you learn specifically why he was determined to ruin the firm and had such hatred for David Lansing?"

He looked at him and said, "You're going to find this hard to believe,

Jacob."

He said, "After all of what you've told me so far, try me!"

"I did promise to tell you when everything had been resolved. Now the case is officially closed. It began years ago after David Lansing had taken over the business from his ailing father-in-law, Claudia's grandfather. According to the account Chatsworth gave me, Lansing played around on his wife Claudette, Claudia's mother. He said everyone knew about it including her, but she never said anything to him about it at least, not that he was aware of. He was always taking frequent trips out of the city, but no one knew where he was going until one day he received an urgent telephone call from his younger sister who lived in another city not far away, asking him if he could pay her a visit. He told her yes, he would come. When he arrived there, she explained everything to him including her pregnancy and, of course, the father's name. He said that he never had the slightest indication that Lansing was involved with his sister. She told him that when she informed him of her pregnancy, he flatly told her to get rid of it because he wasn't going to see her anymore anyway. A few days after that, he received another telephone call informing him that his sister had committed suicide. He never said anything to Claudette or Lansing, but vowed that one day he would make sure he paid for what he'd done. So at that point, he began to formulate his plan by letting everyone believe they were close friends that way. He would be above suspicion when things happened."

Jacob just sat there staring at him in total awe. Then he asked, "Does Claudia know about all of this, Brad?"

He said, "Yes, Jacob, unfortunately, she does now. During our meeting with her yesterday afternoon, she wanted to know why Chatsworth had held such hatred for her father. I hesitated to tell her, but she insisted on knowing the whole truth about everything including

Charles's part in bringing about the business scandal in the first place."

"How is she taking all of this, Bradford?"

"I believe she's going to be all right, Jacob. She's a very strong young woman and she informed Blake and me that she's going to take a few days off to think things through. As for Charles, well, we just don't know because she told us that she'd give her a decision when she returns. But you know, I believe there are going to be some changes made in their marriage."

"My goodness, Bradford, how can one person endure so much disappointment and pain and still manage to maintain their sanity?"

"I don't know, Jacob, I suppose the best way is not to give in but stand fast and preserve regardless of the odds because they can always be changed if we become determined enough and think positive."

Jacob looked at him, smiled and said, "Man, you certainly do have some very interesting cases."

He smiled and said, "This one was mild compared to some I've had to investigate and at least I didn't have to give a deposition in this one."

"Well, P.I., what are you going to do next?" he asked him. He replied, "I informed Blake and Claudia that I plan to stick around for a few days in the event they might need me for something else. And you know, I'm afraid they just might."

Jacob gazed into his eyes and asked, "Bradford, are you thinking that after Claudia has given her decision, she might incur problems with Charles?"

"Yes, Jacob, the prospect of it happening had occurred to me. You see, I've had the opportunity of dealing with him during the investigation and overall, I believe he has a tendency to be quite ruthless if provoked enough. Claudia hasn't spoken it in so many words, but I believe she's aware of her husband's infidelity. Moreover, if that's the case, she just might make the decision to opt out of the marriage. In addition, believe me, that's not going to set well with him."

Jacob said, "I see where you're coming from Bradford and from what you've said, your instincts just might be correct and I'm inclined to agree with you. For now, all you and Attorney Colwell can do is wait until she returns with her decision. If you should happen to be in need of any assistance for any reason, you know how you can reach me."

Smiling, he said, "Thanks, Jacob, it's reassuring to know I have a backup if it should ever come to that."

"Well, Jacob, how are things going with you since all of the excitement is over?" he asked teasingly.

He stared hard at Bradford and said, "You've got to be kidding. There is always something else that has to be investigated in this business and unlike you, I don't have the luxury of choosing all my cases," he said, returning the tease.

By that time, they had consumed their entire meal and just sat sipping on the coffee until Jacob received a call from the station asking him to return. He gazed at Bradford, laughed, and asked, "See what I mean?"

He gave a hearty laugh and said, "Have fun with this one. I'll be in touch." After Jacob left the restaurant, he sat there for a few minutes longer and decided to return to his office. Checking the messages, a call had come in from Blake Colwell asking if he would give him a call, it was urgent. He questioned himself, I wonder what this is about while placing the call.

"Hello, Blake, this is Brad, I've just returned to my office and picked up your message. What's the problem?"

"Hello, Brad, after you left my office yesterday, I was reading David's letter again and I believe in all fairness we should inform Claudia of its contents regarding her marriage to Charles. Will it inconvenience you to come into the office this afternoon, say around one-thirty?"

"No, Blake, it's not an inconvenience. I'm not doing anything at the present anyway, so I'll see you at one-thirty." After the conversation with Blake concluded, Bradford wondered to himself, what has influenced Blake's decision to divulge the information to Claudia now and not before. Something's seriously disturbing him and I plan to find out just what it is!

Bradford arrived at Blake's office punctually at one-thirty p.m. As he entered the front door, He was standing at the desk looking over some papers. He turned around, took a brief look at the clock, smiled and said, "Right on time as usual, huh?"

Bradford smiled back and said, "You of all people, Blake, know how I detest arriving anyplace late."

"Yes, I do, Brad. Shall we go into my office?"

Bradford noticed Jenny the secretary was absent from her desk which meant she probably hadn't returned from her lunch break. Once inside his private office, Blake extended his hand pointing to the large chair directly in front of his desk. Gazing directly into his eyes, he said, "Brad, after reading through David's letter yesterday for the second time, I'm convinced we should inform Claudia of its contents. We don't know what her decision is going to be, but at the least, I believe she should have this information. As for my part, I should have suggested doing just that when were meeting with her. She asked for the truth, but as you're aware of, a great deal of it was withheld. I assumed that her not knowing everything was best, but since thinking it through I feel that I've done her a great injustice by withholding that part."

Bradford stared into his eyes and said, "Blake, I agree with your point that she should've been told all of it, but I believe you only thought you were protecting her from further humiliation. She's going to give us her decision when she returns anyway and as of now, we don't know what that will be. However, whatever the case might be, I feel she should know what happened especially, since she's still married to Charles. Now according to what you've conveyed to me, she's already aware of his infidelity and I'm certain that during her decision-making, she's also going to consider that as well as his betrayal in other areas."

Blake said, "You just might be right, Brad."

Suddenly, the telephone on his desk began to ring, and promptly responding, he said, "This is Attorney Blake Colwell's Law Office."

The caller on the other end said, "Hello, Blake, this is Claudia."

Looking at Bradford, he said, "Hello, Claudia, my dear, I didn't anticipate hearing from you until tomorrow."

She asked, "Is Brad there with you by any chance?"

He said, "Yes, he's right here."

She said, "Because I want the both of you to know that I've made my decision to confront Charles regarding his involvement with Chatsworth in the business scandal that could very well have ruined the firm had not Brad agreed to take the case."

Blake stared at Bradford and asked, "Are you certain about this, Claudia?"

Without one moment of hesitation, she said, "Yes, Blake, I'm certain it's time for me to do this and the sooner, the better."

He said, "If that is your decision then by all means, do it, my dear."

She said, "Give Brad my love. I'll give you a call later."

After replacing the receiver, Blake gazed at Brad and said, "Claudia's made a decision to confront Charles regarding his involvement with Chatsworth in the business scandal. Brad, she is very determined to face him on that issue, and by the way, she sends you her love."

Bradford stared at him and said, "I wonder what his response is going to be when she does confront him."

Blake lowered his eyes to the desk, then, looking at Bradford, he said,

"At this point, I can't even begin to imagine, Brad."

Bradford observed a shadow of deep concern appears upon Blake's face. Again, his instincts began telling him that something wasn't quite right. From the beginning, the clues had been there, but difficult to pinpoint. Moreover, that was becoming an annoyance to him. He believed with great certainty that Blake was deliberately concealing something from him and it has very much to do with Claudia. Precisely what and why was becoming the million-dollar question? Before confronting Blake with his suspicion regarding Claudia, he thought it best to just hold off until they knew what direction she was going to take with Charles.

She thought to herself that she had procrastinated quite long enough. It was time to bring things out into the open. Claudia finally telephoned the firm. Someone else answered the phone and when she asked to speak with Charles, she was informed that he'd left the firm earlier in the day on an out-of-town business trip. Puzzled by the information, she wondered to herself, where could he have gone and why? During their last conversation, there was no discussion regarding any trip. Just what, exactly, is he up to this time, she asked herself.

She telephoned Blake's office and was immediately put through to him by his secretary.

"Claudia, my dear, you sound upset, what seems to be the problem?" "Blake, the problem is Charles," she said.

"What about Charles, Claudia?" he asked curiously.

"I telephoned the firm a short while ago to speak with him and was informed that he'd left earlier in the day on an out-of-town business trip. Have you any knowledge of this, Blake?"

"No, I haven't spoken with him recently. I can't imagine where he might have gone, or why."

"Neither can I," she said. "Listen, I'll speak with you later."

She had just ended the conversation with Blake when the telephone rang. Thinking it might be Charles calling, she abruptly answered, but instead, she heard a strange voice on the other end. It was a recorded message from a hotel confirming the reservation scheduled for Mr. and Mrs. Charles Carrington at six p.m. Standing back with a fixed gaze on the silent instrument, she realized she had just intercepted a message that was obviously meant for Charles. He hadn't expected her to be home. She began to think, so this is something else that he's been up to, further enhancing her suspicion that he was involved with another woman. I wonder just how long he has been playing house. As she sat looking at nothing in particular, her eyes began to swell with tears, but blinking a few times, she refused to allow them to come because of him.

Not a chance, she thought to herself. Whether you realize it or not, Charles, you've just made the next decision easier for me.

Claudia had no concept that in a very short while, her life would be forever changed because she was in for an awakening of her lifetime!

www.ingramcontent.com/pod-product-compliance
Lightning Source LLC
Chambersburg PA
CBHW022101020426
42335CB00012B/778